MISSING

THE FAE THEORY

GEMMA JADE

BEYOND THE FRAY

Publishing

ISBN 13: 978-1-954528-15-4

Cover design: Disgruntled Dystopian Publications

Beyond The Fray Publishing, a division of Beyond The Fray, LLC, San Diego, CA
www.beyondthefraypublishing.com

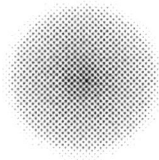

BEYOND THE FRAY

Publishing

This book is dedicated to Damien, Eliana and RJ. My life just wouldn't make sense without my children. You can do and be anything you desire and it's never too late to start building your dreams.
I love you so much.

CONTENTS

ACKNOWLEDGMENTS

I would like to acknowledge first and foremost God and Jesus Christ who, without them none of this would be possible. My mother Carol for always believing in me and also encouraging me to seek out answers and have no fear. My step father Gary for being a bright light of laughter in my life every time I was feeling down. My father Kevin for always being there and helping me back up when I fell, no matter how many times. My husband Ray for putting up with me while writing this book and throughout the process of achieving all of my other, many goals and dreams. I love you. Steve Stockton and Bill Melder for seeing potential in me when no one else did and understanding what I was trying to create. For giving me a platform and helping me navigate both Youtube and real life. I love you both. Thank you for mentoring me and for always being there and being patient. Mary B, Jerome S, Deidre M and Rosalie R and Dr. Reddy at BNBMC; You have all played a huge role in my being able to accomplish my dreams and goals and where I am in my life today. My best friend Donna M for giving me an ear to listen and a shoulder to cry on through my many frustrations. I love you.

INTRODUCTION

Did you ever wonder why, in recent years, more and more people seem to be disappearing from our national parks and other woodland areas around the world? And at such a higher rate than ever before? While many see these occurrences as unexplainable or seem to think they have a reasonable, rational, or even scientific explanation for it all, there are some of us who know better. From UFO and Bigfoot sightings to the bizarre and unexplained clusters of missing people all over the world, no wonder we are left scratching our heads and wondering exactly what is going on in the woods these days. While there are many folktales, legends and theories as to who or what is lurking out there, this book is going to focus on one legend in particular. One legend that I believe can account for a large number of the unexplained missing persons cases. I am finding myself less and less alone in my thoughts, theories and opinions these days as well. We are going to be discussing fairies, or "fae folk."

While most people often think of helpful, beautiful and sparkly, if not a bit mischievous creatures when thinking of fairies, there are others who feel differently. These people are the ones who have heard the real legends, the facts. There are those of us who know the truth about these strange and terrifying supernatural beings. We have heard the tales of the real encounters with them, how bizarre, confusing and frightening they are. When we heard the stories of coming upon one of these mystical beings in the woods, our view was perhaps forever changed. Gone are the days of thinking of fluttering little pixies who sprinkle their glittering dust on you and off you go to a faraway land. Well, maybe something like that, with the sprinkling and being suddenly gone at least.

With all of the craziness in our modern society, it seems it's becoming easier and easier to forget about all of the things that could be even worse going on in the world around us that we can't see. It seems like every time we turn on the television, there is just more and more destruction and chaos. It gets me wondering, "Is this what 'they' want?" Is this all a very carefully carried out plot to take the focus away from the world of the unknown, to make sure we don't get too close to figuring out the truth of what is really going on behind the scenes? The powerful elite and possible government entities whom we are basically indoctrinated to trust since the time we learn to talk don't want us to know or see? What is it they're trying to distract us from? I'm sure the families of the missing could never be distracted from the fact that their loved one was here one minute and POOF, gone the next!

In researching the fae and studying the facts of so many of the cases of the missing phenomena, I had this feeling that I came so very close to touching on something. Perhaps I was so near to lifting or possibly even just thinning the veil that separates the actual truth from the reality we are taught our whole lives to believe. If you are interested in this title and reading these words, it stands to reason that you too are wondering what exactly is lurking in the woods. What is going on out there? In the deep, dark parts of the world's forests and national parks, something is stalking and snatching helpless humans seemingly right out of existence. I think it's worth exploring not only the reality we see right in front of us, but perhaps the hidden worlds of the unknown as well, in the deepest darkest depths of our own minds.

Be careful, however if you aren't familiar with the rules of the deep.

The traditions of legend and lore are still carried out today in the world of the unseen all around us. Before you go on your next walk through a beautiful and silent forest, take that family vacation to one of our national parks, or even just go for a day hike and romantic picnic with the one you most love, familiarize yourself with not only the hundreds of different species of fae out there, but also with the ways in which they operate.

I think it's important to understand here that even the most educated and dedicated researcher on this particular subject could easily be confused by these beings, as it's still unknown what, exactly, they really are. The meaning of the word "fairy," from Latin, is "to enchant; a state/condition/realm of enchantment." There is a common misconception that a creature must be small and frail in order to be considered a type of fairy when in reality some species can be as tall as ten feet. They are like humans in the way that their stature, weight and even physical features are drastically different depending on the individual. While it's true most species all tend to have similar qualities and habits about them, such as the way they dress or certain colors they either always wear or tend to avoid, they range from beautiful to disgusting, fat and skinny, tall and short, smart and not so smart, etc. Come with me now, as we take a walk through the world of the fae, crossing into the realm of the unknown. Let's learn of the sacred truces, bound by blood pacts millennia ago between us and them, and know all the ways those pacts are broken now, about the behaviors and needs of each specific species, and still yet educate ourselves on how not to become another victim or statistic. Let's never leave ourselves at the mercy of anything unknown, especially these tricksters in the woods, who seem to be everywhere and nowhere all at once, just waiting for one of us to slip up and make a fatal mistake.

CHAPTER ONE

CLOSE ENCOUNTERS

Wherever you travel in the world, there seems to be some kind of fairy legend. They differ from place to place, and quite unusually, there seems to be no single point of origin from where they came from or where the stories started. In many cultures it is believed that they are actually demoted angels or even demoted demons who lurk and hide in the woods and forests, ready to snatch unsuspecting victims out of our known place and time, dragging them to who knows where. There is also a strong belief for the need to ward them off using charms of protection, usually worn somewhere on the body. If you ever run into one, be sure not to mention it by name. This will prevent you from accidentally summoning them. Some people who believe in the legends that the fae are in fact some sort of fallen entity, whether angel, demon or other, believe they are neither good enough for heaven nor evil enough for hell below. They can appear and disappear at will, which makes it very easy for them to stalk and sneak up on their targets.

In 1962, a farmer's wife in southern England, reported getting lost in a very remote area of wilderness known to this day as the Berkshire Downs. She recalled not even realizing she was losing her way and became very panicked and confused all of a sudden. She claimed to have never switched course and headed the entire time in the same, and right, direction in which she had originally intended to go. What she realized later on though was that she was actually moving farther and farther into more remote and desolate parts of the land. Away from any other form of civilization. Eventually she got tired and stopped for a few minutes. That was when she heard a sort of murmuring or mumbling coming from somewhere near her, although exactly where she couldn't be sure. Though it was a clear, bright and sunny day, she couldn't see anyone or anything to accompany the strange voice. Suddenly, as she sat there confused and trying to find the source of the small voice she thought she was hearing, a little person stepped out of the shadows of the woods and directly into her path. The bizarre thing here though, the figure she described as "most likely male and dressed all in green" appeared behind her, though somehow she claimed she could see him and knew for an absolute fact he was there. Without saying another word, the little man turned her around and pointed her to the right path, back to her home. The figure then disappeared without a trace right before her eyes, and it was only while talking to her husband later on and recounting her bizarre and seemingly stress-induced experience did she realize she had encountered a fairy. Luckily for her this was one of the helpful ones and not the more commonly known ones who purposely lure unsuspecting wanderers off their track and bring them to places unknown where they will never be able to find their way back.

In Celtic lore, the fae or little people are said to live underground, and any travelers who either knowingly or unknowingly trespass too near these hidden places are said to go missing and are never seen or heard from again. Many people who have reported having an encounter have reported being in a place they had never seen or knew existed before, seemingly in the blink of an eye and with no knowledge or recollection of how they got there. Although this unknown place was definitely not where they were just a second ago, it still was enough like where they had just been to make them question their own sanity. These places are familiar, yet unfamiliar, simply giving one an instinctual feeling that they are somewhere "other." When they finally and seemingly just as suddenly return to where they had left from, assuming that they do at all, always much more time has passed than anticipated. What seemed to them like mere minutes had actually been hours or even days.

If you are looking at legends in the United States, you could always start by exploring the legends of the early Native American settlers. The legends from Mount Shasta seem to be of particular interest to those exploring fairy legends. There were many complaints from even the earliest native settlers on and near this particular mountain from members of their tribes, specifically the hunting parties, who would vanish without a trace, never to be seen or heard from again. This was happening so much, in fact, they started to believe the whole area was cursed. They also spoke of a bright stone that they said traverses the mountain and swallows people whole. They were convinced that this stone had something to do with the fae. Many believe in these legends, the glowing stone and the curse on the area while others believe these were simply scary stories created and perpetuated in order to scare the children, in the hopes of keeping them from wandering too far on and into the mountains alone.

There is a very interesting tale that is said to come from Northern Sweden, from someone whom, out of respect for his alleged desire for anonymity, we will call "Joe." Throughout his childhood, Joe would go to his grandparents' house in a deeply wooded area with lots of trees and trails for a young boy to explore. When he was about ten years old, he and his family went to stay at his grandparents' house for an entire summer. Aside from the one main house, there were a bunch of small cabins on the property, which his grandparents owned, and his whole extended family would stay in these cabins for the entirety of their summer vacations. Joe stayed with his cousins in a cabin that was a little less than a hundred feet away from his grandparents' main house. This was extremely desolate land, and the nearest town was miles and miles away. There was also a lake on the property, and Joe and his cousins' cabin was the closest one to it as well.

There was electricity but no running water, and the family would have to collect their own, as going to the nearest town wasn't a reasonable option for them at the time, as it would have taken so long for them to get there, buy some and then return that it wasn't worth the trip or time to them. Besides, gathering the water and living off of nature like that was part of the fun of the experience, especially for the younger group of cousins, Joe included. While the lake was directly in front of Joe's cabin, behind it was very deep, very desolate woods. Joe's grandfather would tell many stories to the family about alleged encounters he had had while in those woods. Encounters that he didn't know how to explain, as there seem to be no known words to describe exactly what it was he was seeing and experiencing. Joe himself said that whenever he was hiking or simply wandering about in these woods, he always got a sort of creepy and eerie feeling, which he never could explain himself either. On numerous occasions he reported seeing "little people," who would appear and then vanish just as quickly and seemingly without a trace. He claimed that when these little people would cross the dirt paths, anyone nearby would freeze in place until they had gone.

When one of Joe's older cousins heard him telling the other family members about these experiences he claimed to be having, he decided that on the next hike he took with Joe, he would bring it up to joke and possibly tease him about it. Obviously he wasn't a believer. The cousin laughed and pretended to freeze in place while telling Joe it seemed he had come across one of the little people's trails and therefore couldn't move. The boys' grandfather wasn't very happy about this and reprimanded the older boy not to ever joke about the little people, especially not while wandering around in the woods. The subject was eventually dropped, and they all went back to their respective cabins to settle in for the night.

In the middle of the night though, Joe recalled being woken up by some sort of strange noise coming from outside their cabin. The noise seemed to be coming from everywhere all at once, from all around the cabin instead of emanating from one single place of origin. He likened the noise to what he thought it would sound like if bears had been outside scratching on the outside walls of the cabin. It also sounded simultaneously like pebbles were dropping down onto the roof like raindrops and falling down the sides of it. Suddenly though, the scratching sounds seemed to also be coming from underneath his and his cousin's beds, from right there inside the cabin! They were absolutely frozen with fear, "frozen in place" if you will, with terror from the sounds coming from directly underneath their feet. Eventually they summoned the courage to get up and run as fast as they could to their grandparents' cabin to tell them what was going on. No one saw anything outside, they didn't hear anything either once they left the building.

The very next morning, the cousins and their grandfather walked the same trails and paths in the woods they had the day before when the older cousin had made the insult towards the little people, and they scattered candy all along and around those same trails. As they did this, they profusely apologized for offending whatever it was in those woods that night, which had come and paid them a visit they would never forget. Joe thinks it was definitely the little people who had heard them earlier in the day and come to teach them all a lesson in manners and respect.

If you're thinking all of this talk of real fairies has started perhaps with the modern-day version of the "fairy tale" and people possibly letting their imaginations run too wild, think again. Here is a story that takes place all the way back in the seventeenth century. This is an account as to what allegedly happened to a woman named Ann Jeffries. Ann was born in 1626 and passed away in 1698. There was a wealthy neighboring family named the Pitts, who employed Ann as a domestic servant and who were able and willing to verify all of Ann's accounts and claim witness to some as well. Let's travel all the way back in time, hundreds of years, and hear the remarkable stories of Ann's encounters with the fae folk.

The documentation of these encounters came from a man named Moses Pitt, who wrote it all down and sent it to a reverend doctor, Edward Fowler, who was the bishop of Gloucester at the time the strange occurrences are said to have taken place. Moses was seeking the reverend's advice on the matter; this is what he had to say. In 1645 when Ann was around nineteen years old is said to be when the unusual experiences started. Ann had secured a job as a domestic servant for the wealthy Pitt family and began working in their home. While it's unclear exactly how long she had been working for them at the time of the first alleged encounter, we know it didn't take much time for them to start.

One morning after Ann had finished up all of her morning chores, she went into the yard and sat in the garden of the huge estate home. Ann claimed that, while sitting there silently, taking in the nice weather and relaxing on the comfortable arbor, she heard something or someone in the woods very close to her. It sounded as though someone was walking, very lightly, towards her. She thought at first it was perhaps just one of the family members of the Pitts or maybe just a visitor to the home. She quickly disregarded this thought, however, when she began to hear strange ringing sounds coming from every direction all around her at once. Although scared, Ann recalled that the day was so bright and beautiful, she also felt like nothing could harm her. Also, she reasoned, there were people all around her, in front of the house and inside as well. There were many who would be witnesses, if you will.

While the ringing was still going on, and very loudly at that, and while Ann was still trying to regain her bearings, six little men dressed all in green suddenly appeared out of nowhere from the bright and sunny woods nearby. She described them as cute and charming looking with tiny little legs and big eyes. She later started referring to them as fairies. There is no information as to what made her use this particular title for her description or what made her think that this was what these little green men were. Ann said that upon laying her eyes upon them, she became paralyzed or "frozen in place," and after a minute or two she noticed a slight change in the environment all around her before it changed altogether and she saw the little men had brought her to what she called "a castle in the sky."

She said the men "had relations" with her inside this castle.

The Pitt family verified that Ann did in fact go missing for that entire day, and though they searched far and wide, they could find no trace of her. Ann reappeared on her own though, groggy, lying disheveled and in a fetal position on the lawn in the front yard of the home. Ann initially kept quiet about her encounter for fear of being labeled insane or even losing her job. After a while though, she started speaking out and recounting her tale when the fairies, or little men, started to return on a fairly regular basis to repeat the same actions again in the alleged castle in the sky. This began to torment her, and she began opening up to one member of the Pitt family in particular about this harrowing and ongoing ordeal.

Unfortunately she placed her trust in the wrong family member because shortly after confessing that these little men dressed in green were doing these things to her, this person immediately reported Ann to the local authorities, who in short order came and arrested her. She was charged with witchcraft. She was thrown in jail, and the authorities were ready to throw away the key or even condemn her to death. A piece of mail, written by the mayor of the small town where all of this is said to have taken place centuries ago, has been kept and preserved throughout history and can now be found in the Clarendon Manuscripts Archives. This document not only contains verification that Ann was held for quite some time in jail, there is a small portion that seems to back up her claims of the little men's continuous visits to her, even throughout her incarceration. It states how, despite being practically starved for several months, Ann never got sick, hadn't lost any weight and was never even hungry. It was as though someone was bringing her food regularly. Ann herself later told Moses Pitt that the fairies did in fact feed her, by bringing her "unusual bread." The explanation as to exactly what she meant by that was either lost in time or never existed at all. Obviously this wasn't very helpful in proving her innocence or backing up her claim of not being a witch, especially as this was the late 1600s, when it's said a woman who was simply well spoken could be jailed and killed as a witch if her social status was that below someone who the authorities felt should be so. For reasons unknown and never quite understood, the charges against Ann were eventually dropped, and she was released from jail.

After her release, Ann moved on with her life and eventually married a laborer named William Warren. She would later state, while pursuing a new career in nursing, that she wasn't sure how or why it had happened or why they had chosen her, but that the fairies had given her a wealth of knowledge in the medical/nursing fields, and she desperately wanted to use it to help others. She did eventually realize her dream of becoming a nurse.

In 1693, Moses Pitt, who had remained friends with Ann, though he did so in secret due to her being arrested and charged as a witch, decided to send a journalist friend of his named Humphrey Martin to interview Ann about all of her strange encounters and dealings with "the little men dressed all in green," or "the little green men." However, Ann didn't want to talk about it anymore for fear of what would happen to her if word got out again about her encounters. She was quite comfortable and happy in her new life, married to William and with a nursing career, and didn't care to remember any of the torment she claimed to have gone through during her many and frequent encounters in "the castle" but also in jail.

Humphrey Martin wrote to Moses Pitt in response, saying, "As for Ann Jeffries, I have been with her the greater part of the day and did read to her all that you've written to me. But she would not own anything of it. As concerning the fairies or any of the cures that she would perform, I asked her the reason why she would not do it. She replied that if she would discover it to you, that you would make books and ballads of it, and she said that she would not have her name spread about the country in books and ballads of such things." At the time all of this was happening with Ann, in the mid to late seventeenth century, the belief in fairies was very widespread and actually quite common though almost always kept secret for fear of either being jailed or labeled a witch. Perhaps maybe even fear of both, as with what had happened to Ann. There were many reports of these things happening all over the world at the time. Believe it or not, these "castle in the sky" encounters were the most common of all.

I've included these particular encounters here not only because they rang true to me, they fit with everything I've been finding in my research, but also because they are of the most common encounters of the time. Nowadays I know that an encounter involving alleged castles in the sky and strange beings taking us and doing horrific and unmentionable things to us, like making us lose time and then transporting us there and back, are almost always associated with alien and extraterrestrial encounters. Back then in the seventeenth century though, it was very closely related to the fae. Who were, I might add, a much more common being to come across.

CHAPTER TWO

BEYOND FAIRYTALES

It would be completely remiss of us to be speaking of fairies and not mention the origin of so called "fairy tales." Before the written page, the tradition of telling fairy tales was done orally. These stories were reenacted in a very dramatic fashion, such as one putting on an act of a play for another to really get the point of the story across. These tales were not only about fairies but of all types of beasts and monsters that allegedly roamed about the lands where these stories were being told. They were then handed down through generations. Mystical and magical happenings and beings seem to be more a part of the fairy tale itself than actual fairies being included in such legends and retellings. Fairy tales are told solely for entertainment, while the actual mythology of the fae as a whole, in folklore both modern and ancient, is more focused on proving the existence of alleged supernatural beings and phenomena and weaving them into our everyday lives, to be found in the world all around us.

The Brothers Grimm authored the first written collections attempting to preserve the myths, legends and lore as well as the general themes of the tales. The original content written by the Brothers Grimm had to be rewritten several times because the originals had a lot of sexual content and things that just weren't very child friendly. They went through many drafts before coming to an agreement on what would be the final release of their books, making them not only more child friendly but also more profitable. Stories with any kind of troll, monster, hobgoblin, or any other mystical or magical beast can be considered a fairy tale. Some are also tales of warning, meant to keep young children in line by recounting strange, dramatic and most oftentimes horrible things that have happened to other young boys and girls who, for instance, did not eat their vegetables or brush their teeth. Aimed mainly at those kids who didn't clean their rooms or who perhaps told too many lies. After a while anyone writing these fables would be sure to include such a lesson, again not only to make the book more profitable but, also, perhaps to make it more appealing to the parent who would inevitably be the one purchasing it. Do now as I'm sure they did back then and take them for what they're worth to you.

The Brothers Grimm was the perfect name for the authors responsible for such horrific and dreadful books, which were aimed at children of all people. But I want to go a bit deeper into the unknown, if you'll be so kind, and possibly brave, as to join me. There were some really terrible and truly frightening tales told to children back then, again with each one usually having a lesson attached for them to do or not do one thing or another. It's the same today as it was ages ago, really. Be that as it may, I've discovered, much to my surprise, that the lessons in some of our most beloved fairy tales were actually added in, most likely when the real story of what actually happened was taken out. Edited for nighttime stories made to help little kids fall asleep comfortably in their own beds, without waking in the night in a frenzy or terror and running into their parents' room. The actual fact of the matter is, however, that many of our most popular fairy tales do not involve "fairies" at all. They are true stories of real evil. For example, take the beloved brother and sister "Hansel and Gretel."

The story was my favorite growing up and still is in a way. Though admittedly to a much lesser extent than ever before now that I know the true origins of it. The story is set during a great famine, the Great Famine of 1315 to be exact. A time nobody really talks about when we have more recent economic tragedies to dwell on such as the Great Depression in the 1930s, just to name one example. Many people starved to death during this paucity of food centuries ago. Many more died under other, more horrific circumstances, I'm sad to tell you. In their desperation, usually decent human beings carried out acts of extreme cruelty towards their very own family members. Nobody was safe from anybody else. Sadly, parents were getting desperate, and cannibalism against their children and infanticide was rampant. The situation was so critical, dreadful and hopeless, they even left their children to fend for themselves. These children were the lucky ones though, at least in my opinion, when you consider the above mentioned.

Getting back to Hansel and Gretel, whose mother had passed away of some unmentioned thing, most likely a disease or common sickness of the time, and the children were left to be raised by their father. Their father is supposed to be a kindly character, someone who just wanted the best for his children. So he remarried. This is another commonality in most "fairy tales," the evil step-mother. The woman the sweet and good-natured old woodcutter remarries is evil at heart and hates his children, possibly children in general, or so it seems.

When the desperation of the famine hits their village and starts affecting their home, she convinces him to walk his children as deep into the forest as possible and leave them to fend for themselves. He is instructed specifically to make sure they can't ever find their way home.

Somehow, this man decides as well that this would be for the best and carries out the wicked stepmother's sinister and evil plot. I wonder if it had occurred to him his children would surely meet their death. As we know quite well if we are reading this book, there are thousands of ways to die in the woods, or to disappear at least. The father says his goodbyes to his only two children and leaves to go home to his evil wife. Now there will be enough food with only two mouths to feed. This is unimaginable in real life, and somehow "knowing" this is just a fictitious tale somehow makes it more palatable. Until, that is, you remember my words. While this exact story is just that, a made-up tale to try to set the scene of this tragic time in history, this all came from somewhere. Remember, parents did this all of the time during that great famine in the early 1300s.

In this particular story, however, the children stumble upon a whole house made of candy and gingerbread. They are starving and use the last of their food, some stale bread, to leave a trail of crumbs back out of the woods, should they ever decide they want to go home after all, without which they would never have found their way. Upon approaching the house and eating some of its sweet and delicious siding, they are accosted by the evil old witch who owns the place. She takes them for thieves and locks Hansel away while Gretel slaves as a cook all day, serving all of the delicious foods to her caged brother. The witch is fattening him like a pig for slaughter. Inevitably Hansel and Gretel escape. They follow the breadcrumbs that are somehow, a week or two later, still there and hadn't been picked up by birds or other wildlife, and they lead the town to the gingerbread house, which is stocked with food, and nobody seems to care one bit that these children pushed the old hag into her own oven and cooked her. The town feasted on her remains in the original story, and even this part has a sick and twisted origin story.

Allegedly there was a baker during this time who, unlike literally everyone else around her, managed to keep her business going and was not destitute and desperate. She would not be bullied or threatened into giving her livelihood away and ran her bakery as though there was no famine going on right outside its doors. Her name changes depending on who you ask or which version of the story you are telling. Here is how she fits in though, she became absolutely legendary for her wonderful cookies and cakes, mainly of the gingerbread variety. There was another baker in competition with her, a man, and he was in such a frenzy over trying to buy her recipe from her, which she insisted of course wasn't for sale, that he accused her of being a witch. The woman baker was run out of town and lost everything. To add insult to injury, her neighbors and friends convinced her to come back and start baking again. They complimented her and told her how badly they missed her gingerbread cookies. Once she entered the town proper, she was burned to death in one of her own ovens, which she had used to bake the gingerbread sweets. She fed the whole town for at least a day. She never did give up that recipe though.

So how does this all fit in with fairies? Well, it doesn't per se. I was simply trying to show you that every legend comes from somewhere or something in someone's history. Sometimes there is no lesson to be learned, and that's just my point. Why is the word "fairy" in the description of this particular folktale? Why is it in so many others? In my opinion it's because people don't ever want to know the reality of the story they are reading, as most don't dare even try to listen to reason when it comes to learning about the reality of what is all around them. The realities of the fairies and their world, how they interact with us on a daily basis. Perhaps even how they roam the woods hunting us and our children, just waiting for the right moment to strike. So we will never be seen or heard from again.

CHAPTER THREE

MYTHS & LEGENDS

In Ireland there are many theories of origin for these devilish creatures. We spoke a little bit about the thought they may be fallen angels or demons or possibly even the deceased that were unfortunately not good enough for heaven or bad enough for hell. There is another legend, however, one seemingly as old as time, which states that the fae are "certain children of Eve."

According to this Celtic myth, when Eve was in the Garden after having tasted the forbidden fruit and learning she was naked, she hastily decided she must wash her children so they would be presentable in the sight of the Lord when He returned. Well, before she could wash them all, as there were so many, she heard Him fast approaching. She took all of the children left who had not been bathed and hid them underground. Because she and her husband, and presumably all of their children who had been bathed as well, were thrown out of Eden and banned forever because of the disobedience involving the fruit and the serpent, the unwashed children ended up being left behind, left underground to find and make their own way. Obviously leaving children to live in their own underground world without adult supervision could never lead to anything good. It's said though that this is how the first fairy civilization was built.

This legend differs a bit from time to time depending on where and by whom it's being told. It's a bit different sometimes in that it's said that God was simply angry with Eve in general for not keeping her children clean and thought this a sign of great disrespect on her part. Because the children were constantly dirty in His presence, he grew extremely angry and one day took all of them who were unwashed before Him and banished them to live underground, not being able to resurface for at least a thousand years. This punishment would ensure that Eve would never see them again and would therefore be more diligent in making her other children presentable in His sight. Either way, it seems, the children were left underground and to their own devices, fending for themselves somehow. It's said also that they eventually found their way and cultivated a community of mostly little people who are seemingly childlike but who keep some sort of ancient and dark magic with and within them. They are said to hold the secrets to this magic very tightly and at first used it only when there seemed to be no other choice. The more the magic grew, however, the more they used it without a care or concern for the possible consequences of doing so.

Another theory of the Emerald Isle is that the fae are an ancient race that preceded even the Celts in inhabiting the lands we now know as Ireland and England. The Celts are said to have come in and drove these beings off of the land by destroying their civilizations and viciously slaughtering their people, forcing them underground for a time, taking part in a one-sided revenge war for the rest of all eternity. This is why it is sometimes said that the fae have a deep-rooted hatred for human beings, even though most modern-day legends leave that part out, claiming instead that they are mischievous but mostly harmless in their dealings with us.

Either way and no matter which country's legend you choose to set store by, they undoubtedly possess this ancient magic, which no human or other creature on earth possesses and also which cannot be replicated.

Another Irish legend I think you'll find very interesting and which I'd like to recount for you is the one most widely accepted as being the possible reason for connection between the fae and the missing phenomenon, though this is only the surface of it. The legend says that the fae are some sort of interdimensional beings whose universe has somehow bumped up against or intertwined with ours. This seems to make sense for why sometimes we can see them and then in the blink of an eye they are gone again. It could also explain why, once you have been selected and taken by them, you are never seen again. What is underground to us may be the very universe for them, in their world. In all actuality, they may not even really be going "underground" at all, only seeming to, as this is the way they return to their own place and time.

Modern scientists are exploring a lot of theories as to

whether or not these types of things, things such as other dimensions and the ability to travel to and from them, are possible. The general belief so far is that in fact they do exist. While we humans may not yet have the knowledge of how to travel back and forth either within dimensions or through time, that doesn't mean that nothing in all of the universe does. In fact, what these scientists believe they now know in the present moment is that we as a species are very far behind most other dimensions and species out there, of which there are an infinite number, when it comes to themes and things such as these and also in understanding quantum law and so many other things scientific in nature, which, if maybe we could collectively understand it and break it down, who knows what we could uncover. Perhaps we could even recover some of our missing and lost who have seemingly vanished without a trace throughout the centuries. After all, if any of this ends up being true, then it means they have simply just vanished from our sight and plane of existence, and not that they've vanished forever and into nowhere at all.

So what do other countries have to say about the fae and where they possibly come from or even what they possibly are? Where do some of the seemingly endless numbers of legends come from?

In ancient times, it's said to be a well-known fact that fairies actually cared more about the fate of humanity and human beings in general than we ourselves did. This was especially true for human peasants. They are known throughout the world to have cultivated wonderful and mutually beneficial relationships with the fae. The peasants are even said to have worked alongside the minions of the fairy queens, as both she and they cared more about them than any human they had ever worked for or even come across had. As a matter of fact, fairies back in those days, before being driven underground for reasons unknown in these particular legends, were just as likely to be found living in the homes and villages as the humans who lived there.

Sometimes the fairies moved in with not only the permission of the humans who were also inhabiting the home but also with their blessing. They were known far and wide among the poorer classes of the peasants as allies and helpful friends who would use enchantment to keep certain towns, villages or even individual houses where they were welcomed and accepted safe from the ravages of pillagers of the many wars that took place way back when all of this was going on. They are also said to have kept these peasants safe from many of the things they would encounter on a daily basis that could have killed or harmed them. The streets were rife with death back then, in previous centuries, and the fairies were said, for a long time, to keep the poorer classes of humans safe from it all. The fae folk would help to make medicines with their magic to keep the townsfolk and villagers healthy and strong, from becoming sick with one disease or another, as sickness was also everywhere one looked. Sometimes, on rare occasions, they would even bring a child back from death. This was said to have severe consequences brought down onto the fairies by their own kind and usually would cause banishment and excommunication from their own realm, which left them completely at the mercy of and vulnerable to the human race though, so they only did it when absolutely necessary and usually under the cloak of what we would call today a confidentiality agreement or nondisclosure order, which was signed in blood. The punishment for telling and breaking this agreement was not only death but the loss of your very soul to the fairy you had betrayed or their queen, depending on their standing socially with their own kind. The fae were even known to make entire villages invisible to keep them safe from any approaching torch mob or angry army.

When in the woods and forests though, always keep in mind how long ago this all was and how much things have changed. How different now our relationship is with the fae creatures. Don't give any of it even a second thought should you ever happen to be out there and encounter either a fairy itself or one of their many dwelling places. While we are left with only speculation as to why or how the relationship has changed so drastically throughout the centuries, we can be quite sure that it has, and that's really all we need to know.

CHAPTER FOUR

MALICIOUS INTENT

It's often said that humans have simply moved on from how much the fae have helped us in the past, forgetting how essential they once were to the survival of our species. Because of this, some fae species now seek revenge for this perceived wrong. Unwilling to be used and then tossed aside when no longer needed like some old rag, the disrespect they feel and the disdain they have towards the human race, at least in some fairy cultures, could be the reason why they go hunting in the woods as they do, seeking retaliation against all of humanity with the taking of individuals.

There are many different species, breeds and races of fae. There are many cultures, and each different culture holds different belief systems, especially regarding how to interact with humans. It seems as though a change in fairy folklore and even the belief or disbelief surrounding the fae as a whole has changed with every major age in civilization. Some choose to exist on the edges of our vision, wanting nothing but peace and to keep out of our way alto-gether. Keep in mind that no matter how their feelings have either devolved or evolved throughout history, all fairies are known to be either completely or at least a little bit devilish in nature. It seems to be something they can't help, even if they should want to. They can be extremely benign or extremely dangerous, with the latter being akin to what we know today as vampires. These will literally suck the very life force out of every human they encounter and use their knowledge of ancient magic to get rid of any evidence left behind.

There are many different types of reported fairy encounters, and I believe they vary so drastically because generally most people don't understand the differences in the species. What happens to a human once they've come across a fairy depends directly on the type of fae they have encountered.

The first type of encounter and one I come across often is what I like to call the "testing of morality" encounter. If there's one thing almost every single fae legend has in common, it's that they are moral enforcers, which is why they live so much by the code of mutual respect. They will often appear to test a person's generosity and kindness. When thinking about the missing phenomenon, I often think of the young children who tend to disappear without a trace and wonder, after further and more deeply exploring this type of fae encounter, if the fae know the difference between the mind of an adult and the mind of a human child. Keep this question in mind as we move forward. Keep the types of encounters and also the types of people who are reported missing the most and see if you can figure out, possibly, which encounter each group of missing people may have had to experience in order to fail the test and end up missing in this world, or from this plane of existence, forever. If we assume the missing haven't come across an enchanting fairy who will use its powers of magic and enchantment to seduce them to simply drain their life force or blood, to gain their own strength, they may then have encountered the other type mentioned above. The game players or moral enforcers I've previously mentioned.

During such encounters, the fairy will disguise itself as a beggar or some other unfortunate type of fellow who is in desperate need of something the human possesses. Those who help out and are kind and generous will receive blessings from the fairy and perhaps may even have gained a new lifelong friend, or at least a constant protector should they ever need it in the woods again. For example, being led out of the woods or perhaps put back on the right trail if ever lost. But if you are unkind or not helpful, if you show some kind of disdain for the creature and the form it has chosen to take on, or treat it as though it either isn't there at all or not worth your time, woe to you. You will face dire consequences, which include but aren't limited to the loss of your very life! Perhaps even worse, you may be made to be invisible to the human eye and left to wander around, circling the same part of the forest again and again, in some kind of enchantment where there is never a way out, maybe for all of eternity. With your loved ones, authorities and probably search and rescue right within your reach, only you will forever be unable to grasp them. They also will never see or hear you. You are gone to the human realm, only not.

Fairies have been known to bury entire villages in avalanches or drown them in great floods just because of one negative encounter with one unsympathetic human who was a part of it. Could it be that this particular human was just having a bad day? Yeah, but so great is the fairies' wrath and expectation of respect and morality that it wouldn't matter at all the reasoning.

Another type of encounter commonly reported is that of a fae who needs human help in carrying out some sort of work or project it needs done. Should you accept the offer and lend a helping hand, again you will receive some sort of form of blessing in return for your work, despite probably not remembering anything about the encounter at all, let alone the help you gave or what tasks you carried out. However, should you refuse, your punishment would be considered by some to be worse than death. You would be immediately driven into a madness from which there is no escape. Always keep in mind that despite the intention of whichever type of little person or fae species you encounter, they have spitefulness and a mean streak deeply ingrained in them, in the very fabric of their beings. This is especially true when it comes to humans because more often than not, they feel as though we are a species or race who so callously abandoned them once we were released from the throes of poverty and destitution, which made us so beholden to them in ancient times.

In this modern world, at least to most, fairies are

nothing more than a leftover fable, part of outdated children's stories and old wives' tales. It seems as though anyone who believes in their existence is viewed as silly or insipid. Even people who are well respected and intelligent will often be laughed at by society in general and perhaps even lose their whole reputation, becoming known as dim-witted, should they try to lend any credence to the existence of fae and the alleged stories about real-life encounters.

Obviously this is yet another thing that offends and angers them greatly and that they seek revenge for every chance they get. Some cultures, even to this day, believe that most mental illness is caused by some kind of bad dealing with some sort of fae creature. Remember when we spoke about how the fairies and humans lived side by side, sometimes even in the same dwelling, and that the fae still choose to visit human homes from time to time? In fact, some hauntings can even be attributed, at least in my opinion, to an offended little person. The fairy will sit invisible on the shoulder of the person deemed "insane" and torment them day and night without allowing for rest or sleep. They whisper the madness right into the human's ear.

Always be sure to return a favor or kindness given to you by a fairy. They will sometimes randomly show up to offer help when it's most needed in one's life. Perhaps while grieving a loved one or in some form of desperate health crisis. The little person will use their ancient magic to heal the person or provide a deep and almost unnatural sense of peace and comfort to them. They do these things, mostly, without asking for any permission, which techni-cally causes someone to accept their help without even being aware they are doing so. Therefore you will be beholden to and forever indebted to the fae and all the luck and misfortune that will surely find you should you not immediately repay this debt upon it being called in.

There are more types of fae than there are human beings, and the species, races and breeds vary drastically in almost every way, just as each human's looks and features vary despite even being a part of the same family. Some fairies are inherently helpful and kind, while others are downright and wholly evil and deadly. The latter type are known to target specific humans, usually because the smell of certain blood types are appealing to this devilish fiend, or for another reason altogether, which we have no way of knowing or being able to control at all. This type will seek out a person simply to either drink their blood or even drain their life force; this depends on the species of fae as well. They also like to relentlessly torment specific types of humans. Here is where one's mind might wander to the missing in the woods again, as these types are known to be especially fond of bringing the human to the brink of death or existence and keeping them there, as a slave. Doomed to be tormented day and night by the creature who has selected it. After all, just because they are usually much more diminutive in size than we are, we must never forget how strong their magic is. We as a species seem to have lost most if not all of our own ancient magic, which used to dwell within us ages ago. Therefore, the fae are more powerful in every conceivable way than we are, we shouldn't ever forget this fact, but most of us always do. They may not be able to overtake us with their strength alone, but make no mistake, they are much stronger than us not only mentally but magically as well, and for this reason are a most formidable opponent, seemingly impossible to beat.

When thinking of all of the intellectuals who have gone missing on a hiking, hunting or camping trip, I always think of these things. I think of all the knowledge I've gained of the fae, knowledge that I'm sharing with you here now, in hopes the same fate doesn't ever befall you.

Could it be these fae have just happened upon or even specifically hunted down these extremely intelligent human beings, for they have grown bored of playing with the intellectually inferior ones they mostly encounter day to day? Perhaps they enjoy the mental sparring so much, they choose to keep this human with them for a while, using them as some sort of sick experimental plaything, seeing how long it takes to mentally break them down and return them to their alleged previous caveman mentality. Thus draining the human slave/toy of all of their learned intelligence, leaving nothing but their most basic knowledge of humanity and the world itself over a period of possible centuries until there is nothing at all left and they dispose of them.

Inevitably and eventually the human "pet" will die, and the fairy will move on to its next game, enslaving an even more intelligent human being and doing the same thing with this one. We must keep in mind all the while when discussing the fae, too, that time works much differently where they are from. This is evident a lot of the time when someone is lucky enough to return from going missing in the woods. What seems like hours or even days to us humans are mere minutes or even seconds to them. My advice is to keep some kind of iron on you at all times when traversing any woods or forests. Make sure the iron is clearly visible too, especially in the deep woods. This is one of the only things agreed upon by all cultures with even the smallest amount of fae knowledge to even be remotely successful at keeping them at bay. One of the many deeply ingrained powers of humanity is the ability to break the spells, charms and enchantments of other species' magic, especially when that magic is dark and turned against us. Perhaps it's magic, but the same is true when it comes to warding off spirits and creatures like the fae.

There are many symbols, objects and chants that are known to break spells and magical powers, including that of the fae, from humans. These include but aren't limited to rabbit's feet, inside-out clothing, crosses, and believe it or not, pictures of a Japanese emperor, whose name I couldn't find. All of these and more have been known to successfully prevent further or initial magical attacks on humans as well. Some of you may be familiar with these things, and some may not; either way it's definitely something we should all learn and know, especially those of us who spend any time at all in any type of wooded or forest areas. Let's be honest here, even those of us who spend time in our own backyards. The most commonly used way I've found so far to injure a fairy and stop an attack on us is using the evil eye. If you aren't aware of what this is or how to properly use it, it's best you learn, and fast! The evil eye is second to our victory over a fae attack only over galvanized iron, and can stop not just physical but also mental and psychic attacks as well. It's said that some races of fae can't even look upon a human who has iron on their person. Whether it's in plain sight or hidden somewhere, the effect is the same: the stop of an attack that will probably end up being fatal to us had we not come prepared.

When presented with the aforementioned evil eye, other races can't use their magic at all and will be forced to either give up and flee or be at our mercy. Being at the mercy of a human is a fate worse than death to the fae; they will surely disappear when presented with these things the first chance they get. Again though, the tools needed to win victory over the fae depend on its species and how strong their particular magic is. We will discuss this more in depth later on.

CHAPTER FIVE

MISSING IN THE WOODS

Unless a fairy has attached itself to you as a familiar, and trust me, you will definitely know if this is the case, never accept its hospitality. It's completely impossible for us to tell the difference between a well-meaning and helpful fairy who cares deeply for humanity and an inherently evil one who is simply pretending to be so in order to lure you into its web for the purpose of making you either a slave or a snack. Trust me when I tell you you'll never know until it's too late what the fairy has in store for you or what its intentions are.

You don't have to verbally say anything or even acknowledge these small, seemingly benign and insignificant gestures of so-called hospitality either. The only word you ever have to use, keeping in mind this is one of the only times you should ever make direct eye contact with them too, is when refusing and stating very clearly the word "no" when the offer of help comes along. Remember, to refuse a gift or gesture of kindness will be considered offensive and rude and will give the fairy the reason it needs to declare war against you, and possibly any other human who happens to come along after you, for all eternity. Anything other than a resounding "no" will surely be taken as offensive and cause a lot of trouble. In some cases, depending on the intent of the fairy and how they already feel about humans as a whole, it could even be deadly for our species in the generations and centuries to come. As I've already stated, the fae know how to hold a grudge, even the inherently kind and well-meaning ones. So never be insulting or disrespectful in any way, shape, or form, or do anything that could be construed as such by these sensitive beings, unless of course, you are prepared for the fight of your life or the possible loss of it.

Once you have danced with, accepted food from, or even allowed something as seemingly benign as a fairy to brush your hair, you are completely and totally indebted to them. Be sure to keep your wits about you, and don't be fooled. It can be rather easy to be taken in by these charming devils. The well-meaning and friendly, helpful types are harder to come by, as humanity with all of its wars and destruction of the forests and woodlands they call their homes is definitely something that will be on almost all of the fae's naughty lists, and many of them are just aching for revenge. Accepting any type of generosity or favors from a fairy enables them to be able to transport you from our world to theirs, right into the fairy realm at will, in the blink of an eye whenever they should so choose to do so. In this case, even if the fairy you are canoodling with means you no harm, once in their realm, it'll be all the harder for you to protect yourself against any attacks from the more bloodthirsty and depraved types.

So again, unless the fairy is a familiar of yours, and this does not mean simply they have befriended you but more like a witch's black cat type familiar, it will be unable and more than likely unwilling to defend you while in their realm. To do so would have them facing dire consequences and repercussions for their simple hospitable acts. It could even mean a death sentence not just for you but also for themselves, as there is a hierarchy in the fairy world and culture. The higher-ups may see this as them being a traitor, and they will never, under any circumstances, risk their lives to defend or sacrifice themselves for you. They most likely would even be compelled to join in your torture to save themselves and to prove where their loyalties lie. Once we have entered the fairy realm, regardless of how we have gotten there, it's nearly impossible to return to our own world. We will be forever lost, possibly becoming a story in someone's book about strange disappearances or even the subject of someone's YouTube video about the same. There is also a very good chance you will just waste away, as you probably would not ever get back home. Many humans have been doomed to wander between realms, never again experiencing happiness or pleasure, not even on the smallest scale, after having dined, danced or even just spent a little time with the fae folk.

Many who are of the opinion that fairies are directly

responsible for many if not most of the people who go missing without a trace in the woods and forests they choose to explore will tell you that, sometimes, it's just a twist of fate or plain bad luck to have stumbled across a single fairy or, worse, its colony. It can happen, and more often than not, it does happen that without neither the human nor the fairy having planned it at all, either the human will stumble upon it or their paths will otherwise randomly just cross. In either case, it's best not to try to reason with them or explain yourself. As far as the fae are concerned, throughout history humans have been most well known to try to steal their precious treasures, which vary greatly depending on the species of fae, when they claim to have simply stumbled onto an unfamiliar path. Best to just apologize and quickly move along, provided they give you the opportunity.

Perhaps when in the forest, keep a bit of alcohol, tobacco or sweets with you, just in case. Most fairies can be placated and calmed with these seemingly simple gifts. You're most likely to be allowed to leave not only in one piece but in a sound state of mind as well if you have one or all of these gifts on hand, kind of like a peace offering, if you will.

There are certain times, though very limited in nature, when a fairy may truly be in need of human assistance and will therefore try to hire one of us to put in an honest day's work for them. Some examples of this are when a colony of theirs comes under attack, say by a deity, ghost or spirit who wishes to overtake that particular colony, cause general mischief or even kill and overthrow the fairy queen. They will need a human to come around and draw crosses on all of the trees in the forest that belong to them, the places they've made their homes. This somehow allows the fairy to hide inside the trees safely and completely invisible to whichever entity is causing the trouble. It's unknown why humans must be the ones to do this and why the fae can't just do it themselves, but they can't. While it may seem easy enough to help them out in this way, keep in mind how dangerous this could be for the human, as much so as the fairy, because such entities can also attack, stalk, possess, cause great harm to or even kill us or our loved ones. The fae are all but defenseless against the above mentioned entities, which is why they need us in the first place. However, if you succeed in helping the fae hide from these entities, their mortal enemies whom they are completely powerless against, we would be helping to save not only their entire colony but also their queen. You will earn a reward for this help from a Germanic "wood wife," who will present you with a huge bag of lovely scented wood chips. Be sure to thank them profusely and graciously accept this payment regardless of whether or not you find it fair. It's said that when you leave the forest with this treasure, treasure is exactly what it becomes, as the entire bag, every single woodchip, turns into a solid gold piece.

There are stories of mean-spirited and ungrateful humans who have gone out of their way to do some kind of work or another for the fae and refused to accept this most fantastic gift as payment, feeling as though their saving of the queen and/or their entire colony should have earned them more than a mere bag of wood chips, and were very vocal about it. As you can imagine, this did not work out well for that person, as they are said to be currently and since the day they committed this slight against the fae roaming the forests or woodlands where it was done as phantoms, not knowing whether they are coming or going. Never knowing anything of not only themselves but of space and time ever again. Traversing a perpetual circle in the forests, left as prey for any and all other creatures and entities that roam those same forests and woodlands, a sheep perpetually being led to some never-ending slaughter.

The only exception I've been able to come across here is the fairy child, whom we will certainly discuss in future chapters. If you should ever be so unlucky as to stumble across or be sought out by it for some help, just do your best to help it out and expect absolutely nothing in return. They are evil, mischievous and ungrateful, and most have a superiority complex that rivals even the most human-hating and vengeful adult fairy. These little ones are taught that humans are basically their own version of our boogey-man. Whether or not you get anything for your troubles depends solely on the relationship that individual child fae has themselves with the human race. If you should choose not to help or insult the child in some way, whether unin-tentionally or on purpose, you too will end up in the afore-mentioned perpetual phantom state.

One more thing I thought I should mention here is that

the fae will not employ the help of just any human. They do their best to only approach the ones with certain auras and choose what your task will be depending mainly on that alone. Sometimes they get it wrong and, as I said, end up with someone ungrateful and unworthy, but the help they need is not always a matter of life and death. Depending on your aura field, they may ask for your help in cleaning their fields, birthing their children, keeping watch over their own types of livestock or garden, and even, in very rare cases, guarding their queen when none of their own kind who are qualified is available. Although this last one will only happen if and when a particularly special type of human comes along. Some types of fae, and it's usually the ones who do in fact reach out to us for help, are known not only to cause diseases in us but also to cure them as well. Regardless of what the payment is, you should just accept the tasks given to you and carry your work out gratefully. Do not ask or try to figure out what the payment will be in advance, as this is considered extremely rude, and they will not take it well at all. In general, fairies are usually hardworking and proud. They consider it abhorrent for anyone to refuse a hard and honest day's work, regardless of what their payment will be.

Remember, we are also dealing with and speaking of the missing here and how the fairies play a role in their disappearances. I wouldn't be doing my job if I didn't remind you that if you do not know by sight or sound which species of fae you are dealing with, it's best to take extra precautions so as not to stumble upon them at all. If you know what you're doing and don't make any lazy mistakes, it is possible, although very difficult, to not only recognize which species you have encountered, but to escape the situation relatively unscathed. Recognizing which type you are dealing with right away is extremely important because there are some types, such as the Baba Yaga, for example, who will hire a human for menial work with the promise of a great reward once the work is completed, only to give them impossible tasks to complete so at the end of the day there is cause for much punishment or possibly even enslavement. Is this what looks like going missing in the human realm, as you are enslaved in the world and realm of the fae for as long as this despicable creature sees fit? I believe this is what happened to the few who have gone missing for long stretches of time in the forests only to return eventually, either refusing to speak of or not remembering where it was they were the whole while. Perhaps we will never know for sure though. The fae, after all, are known to be extremely tight-lipped, and regardless of how friendly one species may be towards humans, as we say "blood is thicker than water," and at the end of the day the fae will stick with their own kind. It doesn't matter whether they are the same species or not, fae are fae, especially when involving choosing sides between them and humans.

My concern for the missing is ever growing the more I learn about these little creatures of legends and lore we know as the fae. I want to reiterate and you should certainly keep in mind that these are generally not the wish-granting, super-cute and sparkly little lovers portrayed in fairy tales and children's bedtime stories.

They are nasty, ill tempered and cruel and have a great love of abducting humans. It's actually one of their favorite pastimes, making humans disappear. The stalking of the prey being what they love most, the thrill of the chase, if you will. They actually enjoy this part almost more than the abduction/enslavement itself.

CHAPTER SIX

STEER CLEAR AT ALL COSTS

If we revisit the missing phenomenon of all the different types of people who are disappearing in the woods and forests the world over or in the national parks in North America, we can look now at some of the correlation between the parameters that are set up and how almost all of them can somehow be traced back to the fae and their fiendish pastimes. One example is storms and weather events. Fairies are natural spirits of nature, elementals, and can control the elements depending on the type of fairy and which element it is connected with. In the cases of the missing, search and rescue is often stopped and put on an indefinite hold because of some sort of inclement weather event. If you were a fairy who had just abducted some poor, unsuspecting human, would you not use all of your power over the elements to stop that human from being found? At least until you were done with them and had gotten what you wanted and/or needed out of them?

Keeping in line with the elemental facts of possible

fairy involvement in these missing cases, I point you now towards the boulder fields and bodies of water found in the areas where a lot of these people went missing from. In folklore, bodies of water, particularly streams and brooks, which are often found in most forests and national parks, are known to belong to elemental beings, which the fae definitely are, and the element they manipulate the most is thought by some to be water. Boulder fields, on the other hand, are known all over the world as the domains of the fae. You'd be hard-pressed to find a fairy legend where they did not have dominion over all of the boulder fields and small bodies of water in the forests.

There's a very interesting case that happened in the summer of 2015 where a twenty-year-old man who was out jogging with a group of friends ended up missing under strange circumstances and was found deceased later on in a boulder field. The young man and his friends were on a trail in Chilliwack Lake Provincial Park, about 150 miles east of Vancouver. The friends said they were all jogging on their way to Lindeman Lake when Sukhjeet Saggu went on ahead of all of them. They had previously decided to rendezvous at the lake, which wasn't very far ahead of them at that point.

When his friends arrived at the lake, however, Sukhjeet was nowhere to be found. That same night search and rescue in the area were called and immediately sprang into action trying to find him. There were a dozen volunteers searching all along the trail and the surrounding areas. The search was put on hold after some time was spent searching with no luck, and search and rescue were able to get at least thirty people there to resume the next morning.

The head of the search and rescue team spoke about how strange it was that Sukhjeet wasn't found within the usual time span for locating missing people on this particular trail, which was about an hour or two. He went on to say how difficult it would be for someone to actually get lost on the trail. The path the friends were on to Lindeman Lake is well marked and very well traveled. There are hikers there, more than a few, at any given time. Not to mention all of the joggers and runners and people just exploring the area. It struck many of the people involved how strange it was that nobody at all was around to see anything. The trail is never empty, or at least up until this point it hadn't been. Was there something that cleared the area with some kind of magic to ensure there were no witnesses to the disappearance and eventual death? Was it the fae, who saw something in this poor young man they wanted and so desired to do what they do and just take it?

At around two in the afternoon the day after he initially disappeared, a pilot from the Royal Canadian Mounted Police Air Services found Sukhjeet's lifeless body lying in a boulder field located southwest of Lindeman Lake.

Another strange fact about this particular case is how much higher in elevation the boulder field was from the lake. Why and how had Sukhjeet made it all the way up there? He was supposed to be jogging a straight path towards the lake, and with how well traveled the path was, there is no chance he accidentally wandered off it. So what happened here? Obviously I don't know for sure, but I do have a sneaking suspicion that this young man from Surrey may have become a victim of the fae. It sounds like the typical fairy abduction. A runner on a path with a group of people for some reason decides to run ahead the short distance it would take to get to the final agreed-upon destination. The friends show up just a short few minutes later, and their friend is nowhere to be found. Could it be that Sukhjeet was suddenly rendered confused and nauseated by the fae? Did he accidentally wander away, trying to find a place to rest? Did the sudden confusion lead him to forget where he was going altogether, and again, did he mistakenly climb and then fall into a boulder field? My opinion is he was lured specifically to that spot. Normally in cases where someone goes missing near or in a boulder field, they are never found, usually leaving something behind like an article of clothing or perhaps their sneakers. I've included this case because of how familiar the story is, but also how bizarre the differences are. There isn't much information I could find on Sukhjeet personally, and my condolences and deepest sympathies go out to his family.

Not only in line with the missing, but also in UFO and Sasquatch/cryptid-suspected disappearances, you will find a general refusal from most animals, search dogs in particular, to venture into woods which at any other time they would've explored without hesitation. These dogs are usually trained to search, rescue and hunt; however in so many cases of the missing we find that the canines just absolutely refuse to do the job they were born and trained to do, a job that at any other time they would have loved. The dogs are scared, plain and simple.

When looking into much of fairy folklore, you will see precisely why this happens. This behavior is not only rife in fairy lore but also becoming more and more common in each missing persons case we come across where a search and rescue canine was employed. The same is true for the missing's pets, which unfortunately accompanied them out into the wilderness and most likely witnessed the fairy abduction. The dogs are afraid of the fae, as, I reiterate, they are nasty and mean little creatures and sometimes put a hex of confusion on the poor mutt, making it chase and bite its own tail. Sometimes they will go so far as to invisibly injure the animal, either physically or mentally depending on the fairy's mood and intent for that particular abduction.

That's right, they use fairy magic and play a game with their children, sort of like the human version of pinata, only with magical needles that make the animals bleed but leave no mark. I won't explain further; just use your imagination.

The next connection I want to help you to understand is one many find the most creepy of all, the disembodied sounds heard by search and rescue people and volunteers. They will hear disembodied screams for help or moaning sounds of pain coming from somewhere... From nowhere deep in the wilderness. The issue? The sounds are the voices of the missing individuals they are currently out searching for. The person is already enslaved by the time the searchers come to the rescue, remembering the inclement weather and refusal of animals to hunt, which buys the fairy more time to capture its victim. And perhaps to hunt them and have their fun for a little while longer. By the time the fairy lifts all of these magicks, it's too late.

Though the victim hasn't figured that out yet and still clings to the hope he or she will be heard, not knowing they are already lost forever. Doomed to a life of slavery worse than anything imaginable, worse even than death.

This reminds me of an encounter I heard of a while back about a woman who was hiking alone in the woods and got lost. In trying to find her way back, she had injured her ankle and found it impossible to do anything more than crawl around. She knew she would never be able to make her way out, not with the severe injury she seemed to have suffered. Eventually too, she realized that even if she wasn't injured, she most likely wouldn't have been able to find her way back to her trail even if she was able to get up and walk around. She was lost, having no idea where she was or how she had gotten there. The trail she was hiking was one she had traveled a hundred times or more, which was why she felt so comfortable going by herself for the hike in the first place. She knew she had to find a place to sleep for the night, as it would be at least a full night before anyone would realize she wasn't back yet and start searching for her.

She crawled her way underneath a large tree, trying to keep herself warm and dry until her friends sent someone to find her.

The next morning she heard the search party calling for her, and full of relief, she started responding and calling back. Despite being able to see the searchers only a couple of hundred yards away, they seemed to not be responding to her at all. It was almost like she was invisible to them. This went on for three more days until finally, five days after initially being lost, the search and rescue teams, who were just about to give up and who were going over again the spots they had already searched, one more time, in case maybe they found her this time actually did. They saw her lying under that tree, and finally it seemed they had heard her cries for help. They found her, and she had quite a story to tell.

She later recounted how she was suddenly feeling very sick. She was confused and dizzy and couldn't keep her head up. She presumed this was the reason she had gotten so far off her path. She claimed to have fallen off a small cliff and landed directly on her ankle, which later was found to be completely shattered and needed several surgeries to fix it. She claimed that during the nights, as she lay under that tree trying to sleep and rest despite the excruciating pain from her ankle, she started to see something terrifying. Night after night there were beings all around her, watching her silently.

They did nothing but pace and stare at her; the energy emanating off them was pure evil. She also reported that, aside from these shadow-type entities who were faceless except for the glowing eyes, there were other creatures there as well. She said there were tiny little men, the size of those gnomes some people put in front of their house or in their gardens. These tiny men were bringing her "strange bread" and seemed to be warding off the evil shadow beings. She saw neither of these creatures during the day; only once the sun set did they come out and interact with her. The whole while these silent shadow beings just stared, stared and grinned.

Once the morning came when she was finally rescued, she claims that the little men made a circle around her, and something very strange happened. She would recall that she saw something like a bubble lift from on top of her. A kind of shimmery haze had made a circle all around her, one she hadn't noticed until just then. Though these little men didn't speak, she somehow knew they were there to set her free. She also instinctively knew that the shadow beings were the ones who had lured and trapped her there, most likely for some horrific purpose she would rather not think about.

So what happened to this woman? It sounds to me like she somehow stepped or was lured into some kind of portal. Was she transported to the realm of the fae? If so, why did they help her? It's always been my opinion that there are portals everywhere, especially in the deepest darkest depths of the woods and forests. Some lead to alternate dimensions and realities, and some lead to unknown realms, like that of the fae. We may never know why they helped her or why she was able to eat the bread they gave her without being forever changed, as I mentioned one always is when eating fairy food. These are the questions I hope my research will answer for me someday. For now, all we have are a bunch of maybes, which is good enough for me.

Ever wonder why some people turn up dead and some

are lost forever, never to be found, not hide nor hair of them? Well, the explanation for this is actually quite simple for anyone familiar with the fae and their ways. See, it's all about usefulness. Who of the humans will pose the biggest challenge to them? They don't, for example, want to hunt someone who isn't gonna give them a run for their money. This is also why people who are extremely smart and very athletic, even avid hunters, are almost never found and lost in the blink of an eye. The fae wants a challenge! After they've played enough, it's time to test the human's intellectual strength and/or physical prowess depending upon their particular need for that particular slave for that day. If the person proves to be useful, either physically, intellectually or both, the fae will keep them. If not, they will be killed and returned to our dimension, our realm, if you will. The reason places are searched dozens of times just for the person to turn up days later in the exact same spot is because the fae was kind of interviewing them, if you will, only not for a job, oh no! They were being interviewed for what kind of slave they'd best make. After it's decided they are useful, they will be magically transported into the fairy realm, never to be seen or heard from again.

Every once in a while, a mischievous and especially cruel fairy, usually a child or young adult, will place articles of clothing here or there simply to watch the searchers find it and get a renewed sense of hope. They then stand by for days, watching and waiting until they see those hopes suddenly dashed upon the realization that they would find nothing more. The reason for the constant and seemingly random shoe finding? Simple; aside from the smaller species who use them as homes, which we will get to in a later chapter, the fae are extremely clean folk, and shoes are very, very dirty. Especially after someone has been chased through the forest.

The last of the most common focal points, or parameters, that are found in so many of the disappearances of the so-called missing person phenomenon I want to discuss with you here is the berry picking. This is the simplest of all the explanations, which is why I chose to do it last. Berries that grow in the forest are considered by the fairies to be their own food. They love the delicious and plump seasonal fare that grows all over some bushes near water. They collect and store them (in case of a shortage of human blood that year, maybe?), and therefore to simply pick a berry, let alone dare to taste or eat them, is considered thievery to the fae and will be punished by eternal enslavement or possible death.

CHAPTER SEVEN

THE ALMOST MISSING

Now that we have covered what I consider to be the most basic parts and elements of the fae and their connection with the world's missing in the woods, the strange and nonsensical deaths and disappearances, I'd like to explore much deeper, and possibly much darker, into the scary world of the missing and the fae. After all, let's also not forget that the fae are supernatural and they precede humanity; therefore so much about them is still unknown to us.

From what we do know, fairies are actually some of the most frightening and dreadful creatures a human could ever encounter, especially in the deep, dark depths of our world's forests and woodlands. And let's not forget our national parks. Fairies are magic, and magic in the wrong hands can be deadly. Could fairies at least be a part of the reason why people all over the world are going missing in the blink of an eye and vanishing without a trace? Fairies are reportedly seen everywhere and anywhere. Wherever there are boulder fields and berry patches, streams of water and circles of stones. Their places of dwelling, if listed, could go on and on. Don't let their mostly small stature fool you, fairies themselves are magic, and they know how to use it.

For better or worse, for good or bad, for life or death. This fact alone makes them so much more formidable than we recognize because of how tiny we have all falsely come to believe they are.

I'd assume that by now you know enough to never set out and seek something that you don't understand and couldn't possibly even begin to comprehend, such as the fae, but let's just say you are unfortunate enough to happen upon a fairy during a day hike or camping trip.

Completely innocently and by accident. Remember to never give them your name, for this gives them power and possibly even complete control over you. Perhaps give them a fake name or even a nickname, and remember, if you know their name and say it aloud so they can hear it, they must leave you alone. Who knows why? It's simply a law of nature as far as the fae are concerned.

When trees die, sometimes rings of wild mushrooms sprout up in their place. Many believe this is where the portals to the fairy realms lie, inside these mushroom rings, these fairy rings. Never stand inside one. Upon first hearing this, I couldn't help but wonder if maybe this is one of the reasons why people are going missing as well. Being lost in the woods for days and sometimes even weeks, a human being is going to get hungry. Someone dehydrated, confused and most likely delirious and possibly even hypothermic isn't going to be thinking straight and may see these mushrooms as food. Is this another lure? Are the fairies themselves what are making these people suddenly sick and needing to separate from the group, only to find themselves confused and lost and not knowing even sometimes who or where they are?

Maybe they suddenly come upon these mushrooms and in their discombobulated state decide to eat them. Who knows, maybe the fairies even put it into their minds to do so. They then enter the fairy realm, and who knows what is done with them. Most likely their loved ones will never see them again. Mushroom rings equals fairy traps. Lesson number one.

There are many special types of phenomenon that come along with a fairy encounter. Sometimes a person will experience just one of these things, and other times they'll experience two or more, sometimes all. One thing we've been hearing more and more about in the stories of what I like to call "the Almost Missing" is a profound silence suddenly coming upon nature right before the encounter. A kind of static will enter the air as well, leaving all of the hairs on your body to stand completely on end, an electric charge like right before a loud and particularly violent storm. There will be a sense of losing time somehow, of course with no way of knowing why or how the time was lost and sometimes even where it went to. Many people report, while experiencing a fairy encounter, one they thought they had just happened to come across randomly, whether to their great or terrible luck, there's a sense in the back of their minds somehow, perhaps even in their subconscious, that whatever display they're witnessing is being put on just for them, as though maybe it wasn't such a random or chance encounter after all.

There's always either an unusually clouded or unusually vivid memory of the experience, and you could also start to feel as though this particular sighting or event happened at a very specific time in your life, as if it were fate somehow with the fairy encounter somehow marking a turning point in your life. These are just to name a few of the feelings and physical experiences one may suffer before, during or after encountering a fairy or fairies.

Of course, there can be some form of reconciliation for us, once we come to the conclusion finally that the old legends of beautiful beings fluttering about on gossamer wings and drinking dew off of beautiful tulips are nothing more than made-up lore, fairy "tales" if you will, told to lull us into a happy sleep and give us even happier dreams when we lay our little heads down at night. At least that's what I always thought the purpose of such nonsensical stories were; however, now I know better. It is of the opinion of many experts on fairy legend and lore that perhaps these stories were made up by the fae themselves in order to cause those who hunt them to think them more harmless and unassuming. This reconciliation being that we do not have to toss these old legends aside completely and come to know the fae in a different light; perhaps they'll become even more enchanting to us, even as we become more aware of the danger associated with and all around them.

We've talked before about many of the parameters

used when deciding which cases of missing people fit into the completely baffling, those that have no other explanation at all than something we humans may consider otherworldly. We know the fae are much more commonly reported as being seen than angels or even demons; however, we still know much less about them. We know they're misunderstood for sure, keeping in mind again, what we've always been told about them and what's actually the truth. When a person goes missing, all we really have to go on is either the scant evidence left behind (if there even is any), or the testimony of the people who, for whatever reason, were allowed to come back. Yes, I use the word "allowed" here because there's no way of escaping the fairy realm without permission. Once you have entered a portal, even by complete misstep or accident, you will be trapped there forever unless you are granted permission to leave.

In speaking of all of the many types of different fairies some of the missing may have encountered right before they vanished, the mind may begin to wander to all of the "causes of death," all of the ways we try to be reasonable and rationalize the way in which some of the people were said to have met their end while in the woods. We've talked so much about the hideous and unimaginable creatures some of the fae folk actually are, but there are also several species who are inherently beautiful and charming. I wonder if it's even more likely that it was some of these types who have led many of the missing to their own demise.

CHAPTER EIGHT

EXPLORING THE DIFFERENT SPECIES

When exploring how many of the deceased bodies of the missing who are eventually found are said to be hypothermic, I can't help but be reminded of the Asrai fairy. Similar to, but not the same as a mermaid, the Asrai are incredibly beautiful but quite shy. They are mostly nomadic creatures who aren't all inherently evil, but tend to be sometimes. The touch of the Asrai's hand, however, will cause the human's skin to become so very cold, it can never feel warm again. Thus possibly inducing the hypothermic condition that is said to be responsible for many of the missing who are later found deceased under strange circumstances. Although said to only surface once a century, it's not certain how long this once-a-century visit is for. Who knows how many victims it has time to take from this earth.

As mentioned earlier, we sometimes receive stories from those who were missing for periods of time, and sometimes those stories tell of being misled while trying to find their way in the woods. We already know fairies are made of magic and can use it to bend humans to their whims. When I think of the delightfully mischievous pixie, I can't help but wonder as well, if this isn't the fairy the lost traveler comes upon. These little troublemakers mislead traveling humans about where they should next go, about which path to take to find their way to where they are meaning to end up. This is like sport for them, most of the time it's done telepathically, but every once in a while, you will hear the stories of Disneyfied pixies whispering in a lost traveler's ear. Be very wary of their beauty and charm, for nothing they utter ever seems to be the truth, it's simply how they're made. Are they working in tandem with other magic or unseen forces and/or beings in the woods and forests, helping these others to lure a hapless and unwitting human in? That's something else to add to the long list of things we may never know. Well, some of us may find out, but it's doubtful we will ever be able to speak of it again. Remember, pixies are said to be changelings. Instead of working with another being or creature, could they BE that very thing?

Do they play a sick form of manhunt or tag with each other using the humans? Some wonder if the infamous Flannel Man is in fact just a shape-shifting pixie.

In the previous chapters of this book, we have learned so much about the fae, yet we still haven't even scratched the surface. We often wondered why the fairies would ever need a mere human for anything so serious to keep them longer than the time it takes to get some quick chores done, a very simple interaction. There is a type of fairy that desperately needs humans in order to continue breeding, to save their own race. This would be the classic elves.

Elves are said to be half human after all, and they can only go so many generations without a human being donating some DNA to their bloodlines before they become extinct. Endowed with a sense of excellent hearing and sight, they are also quite graceful and charming when they need to be or when it will serve them. Don't be fooled with the knowledge of how these little ones possess a natural defense against any and all dark arts and black magic. Simply because they possess it, that doesn't necessarily mean that they ever use it. Though I'm sure, just like humans, all forms of fae folk, all species, have their good and bad attitudes.

Another species of fae who are said to have superior physical beauty are the merpeople. This, of course, depends on who you ask, as in recent years humans believe they have come to know that these species of half human and half fish would have fangs like a piranha and no need for hair, even the females. However, let's suppose for a minute that what most of the old research said about these merpeople is in fact accurate. Let's imagine for a moment they are aesthetically pleasing and almost too beautiful to look directly at. They are known to be the ones who lure sailors and seamen to their deaths. The female's enchanting beauty is absolutely irresistible to the human man. These half-fish half-human bombshells must do this sometimes to save their own species as well. While we are simply speaking of the missing in the woods, I'll move on. But make no mistake that these sirens are just waiting for some poor fisherman to cross their path. Think of all the missing who have ended up in water and were never captured on any cameras going in, with no eyewitnesses either. Could it be a form of merperson? Of course it cannot be the seawater-dwelling type, but who could ever really know all the possible types and species of any creature if we can't even prove the fabled ones exist. After all, all merpeople are said to be able to manipulate water. Who's to say there isn't a type that dwells in lakes and regular unsalted bodies of water and does just this to their unsuspecting victims? Taking them as slaves? We just can't say; we may never be able to either.

This next entry may surprise some of you, depending on which of the many legends you've heard of the banshee, the Irish legend of the wailing woman whose vocals warn of someone about to meet their demise. Depending on which tale you're familiar with, the banshee is either a beautiful enchantress or a raggedy old hag. Regardless of what she looks like, no household or member of it can escape her torturous wailing. When the banshee comes a-calling, her looks aren't going to matter. She is one of the more mysterious types of fae. Many believe this is because she has been only recently classified as a member of the fae people.

Only now is more research being done into what the banshee's connection to the fae realm is and what sort she may be.

Not every single species of fairy is inherently mischievous, malevolent or evil. There are very few exceptions, sure, but exceptions there are. Take the brownie, for example. Have you ever wondered about all of the people who have survived such rough and exhausting weeks and months even in the deepest darkest parts of the woods and forests, only to have some strange story of miraculous survival. Well, could it be the brownies? Brownies get their name from their brown skin and hair. While not visible to ordinary people (only those with the second sight are said to be able to see these little ones), they are able to shape-shift into anything they like. They are another breed of changelings, and although they usually take the image of farm or domestic animals when doing so, they sometimes take on the form of what or whoever the person lost or ill would be most comfortable with. Even staging the meeting sometimes as a hallucination, putting the human in a kind of dream state, so as to blur the lines of memory lest they discover it was in fact a brownie who had healed them and nursed them back to health before sending them on their way to safety. Perhaps even protecting them from the other, more mischievous and dangerous types of fae creatures.

Remember that the legends of the fae come from every culture all around the world. Is this just a coincidence? That every culture dating back to the beginning of time has had some sort of legend regarding some sort of fairy type? Probably not! It's probably because they actually do exist, just the sightings of them are being reported less frequently.

CHAPTER NINE

THE EVANESCENCE OF THE CHILDREN

In general the fae folk and their rules are very different from ours, and we will most likely never be able to figure out or even understand all of their little idiosyncrasies. If the more benevolent and perhaps mischievous types can cause so much damage as mentioned above, how about the other more dark and sinister types? What role could they possibly play in these missing and vanishing events happening all over the globe these days? In the wilderness, most times, all of the elements of the earth seem to come together, yet remain separate. The streams and ponds feed the soil, which grows the plant life, which gives life to the air, and to us humans.

Sometimes even the inclement weather or some other force causes there to be fire. Almost all fairies tie themselves to one element in particular and usually do not travel outside the bounds of that element. If they are the type to typically travel in groups, they will do so with members of their same element. What are some of the more hurtful and perhaps vengeful types of fae species, and what are their possible roles in what's going on lately? We talk much about alternate dimensions and perhaps the missing crossing accidentally into another one while lost and trying to find their way. Sometimes even being led or compelled to do so by an outside force, fairy or otherwise. It's true fairies usually live close to humans, however their dwelling places are always distinctly separate, and most of the time they are on a plane or in a dimension even right above, below, or parallel to ours.

There are many legends out there about the fairy "raids." Remember, science wasn't nearly as advanced in previous centuries as it is now, and while all of this was going on, most people who were considered educated, such as physicians or scientists, didn't believe in such "nonsense" as fairies. When the fae would do one of these raids, or "rides" as they were sometimes called, through the countryside, normally it was because they were looking for one thing in particular—human children. These rides would happen mostly when there were a handful or more of women who had just given or were about to give birth in one village. The fairies wouldn't hide in the shadows though like they do today. They made it well known they were coming, they were there, and what they wanted. Whether or not they visited your house to steal your already born and healthy child or left you alone was really based on sheer luck. There was nothing you could do to stop them; after all, who would you turn to? Anyone who was considered "well-bred" would have you committed as insane should you report to the proper authorities your child had been stolen by a fairy or switched to a changeling, and this is exactly what the creatures counted upon.

Sometimes the fae would also curse certain people, certain homes with pregnant women that the minute their child was born, they would hand it over to the fairy and not remember a thing. Much of the time, the healthy newborn human would even be switched with a sickly and pale fairy changeling, and the parents would be none the wiser. They did this by leaving some sort of charm or totem in the home, which the parents knew nothing about. Again, even if the parents were to find the totem and remove it, remembering that the child they are caring for isn't theirs, what could they do? We will discuss later how one could possibly get their own child back. This practice of switching is a lot less common these days for obvious reasons. Although, it's still the same when I stop and wonder if this were to happen, even if I were 100 percent sure, who would I tell? I would probably be arrested for child neglect or have my child taken on the grounds I was crazy in thinking they were a changeling. In some cultures though, a person might be believed and be given ways to get their own child back, but this is so rare, we would probably lose our children forever. This is why we must always have our eyes on our children at all times, especially in the woods. Fairies who are looking to switch a changeling with a healthy human are looking mostly at babies and children three and under.

The REAL changelings, as in fairy children that have been swapped for a human child, are one of the more terrifying types of malevolent fae. While technology has made it almost impossible for fairies to go around swapping their babies with human ones, it does happen every now and again. The child, as it grows, will always have trouble fitting in. Not only will they always be more beautiful than the rest of the children their age, but they will also have trouble relating. This leads to a life of constant isolation, which can make some of them snap. Could this perhaps explain a whole other type of human problem in society for the past few decades or so? The child murderer, the child who kills? That's not what we are here to discuss today, but maybe another time. Another time indeed.

Devas are tiny fairies that resemble fireflies. In fact, if you live or are in for whatever reason a wooded area, you've almost certainly come across a deva. Known to hang around well-cared-for plants and to flutter far away from decaying or dying flora in the wilderness. Is this what entices the flower pickers who go missing from time to time? Could be. Are these the creatures who either intentionally or otherwise lure the little children into the woods, never to be seen or heard from again? Picture it! A small child chasing a firefly to collect it in a jar and keep its light for a few minutes. As the deva or firefly flies away, away, away... so the child roams and follows. Maybe never to be seen again. Maybe, perhaps, to be kept in a fairy child's jar, where its cries can be kept for a while, until the fairy child loses interest, as the human child does after a while of the firefly's beautiful glow.

Another almost epidemic-like problem happening with the missing in the woods nowadays it would do us well to spend just a little more time on is the missing children. Not the ones who return to tell the tales of their grandmother being a robot and taking them underground. (While that WAS a very interesting story!) No, I'm talking about the ones who never return, like Dennis Martin disappearing not just without a trace but seemingly into thin air. Right off the face of the earth... Out of existence. Or so it seems.

It would be reasonable to assume that the Bendith y Mamau is the culprit in many of these cases. This translates to "mother's blessing." Could it be possible that the fae see themselves this way? These lesser known fairies who indulge in the nefarious act of actual kidnapping. At least that's what we as humans call it. These are the fae who are usually responsible for the aforementioned changelings. They have a nasty little habit of taking healthy human babies and leaving their own, "not so healthy" little "crimbils" in the human child's place. This is what they call them, the fae, they call them "crimbils," the replacements. Parents of the pilfered child have to consult a witch in order to get their offspring back. Sometimes though, as strange as it may sound, the fae folk actually return the child on their own, but only after they instilled in the child a great love and appreciation for music.

Perhaps this is another one of the many reasons for so many children seeming to vanish without a trace from right under their parents' noses while out in the woods. There are many stories of young children, usually but not always too young to speak, being found safe days or even weeks later and being either unable or unwilling to tell what happened to them or where they went when they were gone the whole time. When they can and will tell the story, it's always chalked up by the adults to an overactive and perhaps scared imagination of a child trying to reconcile themselves to something absolutely terrifying having happened to them. I'd like to think that by now we know better, those of us who research the subject of the fae and how they operate. I'd like to think that stories of bears and wolves caring for the children for the duration of their lost time is often very believable and even simply explained. The fae who are able to shape-shift took the child or lured it, for whatever reason, and decided it would be okay to send it back. If any of our species are lucky enough to be returned from the fairy realm, it is definitely the innocent children, at least when it comes to a small percentage of the more friendly and benevolent types of fae. Of which, I can tell you without a doubt, there aren't many. Anyone who returns is incredibly lucky to do so at all, even more so if both their bodies and minds are still intact.

CHAPTER TEN

LOW FAE ON THE TOTEM POLE

Even the most educated and dedicated researcher could easily be confused by these beings we call fairies, as it's still unknown what, exactly, they really are. The meaning of the word "fairy" (from Latin) is "to enchant; a state/condition/realm of enchantment." For centuries humans and fairies existed side by side, sharing the earth and all that is in it. Humans are even said to have been involved in trade with the fairies and had daily interactions with them for numerous reasons. Unfortunately since mankind has become so ruinous, the fairies are said to have been losing their powers. They were originally given dominion over the woods and the streams inside them. They basically ruled over all of which is now called "mother earth" until we started destroying the forests and breaking the sacred truces that were created millennia ago. Mankind's need for answers has had a devastating effect on all species of fae as well; our constant experimentation on them has turned them into an enemy. A very formidable one too.

While we have a general idea of what the fae are and are learning about all of the different species and the ways that we shouldn't ever provoke them, unfortunately sometimes we can do so unintentionally. Many are convinced this is one of the things happening in our woods and forests, our national parks too, to the people who end up missing. Are they accidentally crossing unseen boundaries or traveling to unknown lands? Are they inadvertently breaking the aforementioned truces between humans and the fae, agreed upon in the beginning of time? It's rumored we have driven them off of their own land, perhaps even underground. Could this be why they are seeking vengeance? Some even say the fae are coming after us humans because they have a very strong sense of justice and righteousness, which is offended by our constant pollution of their home in the woods of the world. Is it their hatred of human deceit that made them become so uncharacteristically vindictive, spiteful and even in some cases violent? Do we have that much influence on them?

As we walk through the realms of the unknown and into the world of the fae, do not cross slowly. Watch carefully what you come across, as what you see with your eyes may not actually be what's real. Should a fairy dressed all in red approach you and slap you about the body, surely you will die. Woe to anyone who should try to remove you from their grasp or clutches even after death. Once a fairy claims you, you are rightfully theirs, at least that's the way they see it. A person looking to investigate the effect the fae have on, or what part they play in, the world of the missing will find something drastically different depending on which culture's legends and lore they are looking into. In order to understand the way they work, one must know how things are done where they're from. I don't mean just learning how not to offend their delicate sensibilities or which treats to leave which type you should come upon should you find yourself in their bad graces either. Let's explore their world a little bit and see where these legends may have come from, and what possible connections they could have to all of the missing people popping up more and more frequently in today's news.

It's a little known fact that the fae also have a very complex hierarchy and even have kings and queens who rule over more than just their own species. There are certain types that cannot rule and are "the low man on the totem pole," for lack of a better term. For example, goblins.

Goblins are pests who work at the behest of greed. They always travel in pairs but never in groups; it seems they can't stand to be around each other any more than the other kinds of fae can stand to be around them. They are grotesque and one of the smaller species of fae. They are not only mischievous but hostile and won't hesitate to attack a helpless human walking alone. They are led by greed, not for money as some humans and other types of fae are, but for gold and jewelry. Are we checking to see if there is any jewelry taken from the missing in the woods? Though small themselves, they are larger than the average toddler, mainly in girth. Part of what makes them so disgusting is they do not clean themselves except to bathe in mud and muck, the dirtier, the better. They stink to high heaven and are cowards. I say this and have mentioned a smaller child because, well, when a child goes missing in the woods, this is the species of fae I always think of first. They usually won't go after anyone in a group and tend to make themselves invisible to the human eye and run off when there is more than one of us taking a hike or even camping. However, if you should be traveling alone on a hike or if you should not be keeping a close eye on your child, beware, for a goblin will sneak up on them, and before they can even see anything there, they'll be gone.

They are not smart at all though, so a child perhaps wearing something that glitters or shines in the sun may inadvertently be attracting these vile little monsters. Once the child or lone adult is in the clutches of the goblins, they'll be searched head to toe and inside out for gold and jewels. Woe to the hapless victim should they not have any, for their fate could be worse than death. While goblins do mate and reproduce, they are the only species of fae that can turn a human into one of their own race. This is most likely why many children are never found.

These are the goblin's favorite prey because it isn't a challenge. They are slovenly and sickeningly obese, oftentimes slow and lazy and despise a challenge. Should your innocent child cross their paths, they will surely be frightened and can probably outrun the monsters, but if they don't, they will most likely be turned, their humanity and innocence gone during the transformation. They will be brought to wherever the goblin's lair is, whether in this realm or another, and they will never be human again nor have any memory of ever being so. Though such things would be a violation of the ancient truce between us and the fae, so much we have done is a violation that the goblins will usually not see too much trouble for what they've done.

The fae, as we have come to know, are spiteful and wicked, for the most part at least, and even the ones who aren't won't risk themselves to speak out against such atrocities done to us humans, even our children, who are usually off-limits to all but the goblins and the changeling elves.

Aside from lusting after our human gold and jewels, there is one type of goblin almost worse than the regular ones we just discussed. These are the "Red Hats." All goblins wear pointed hats, just like the gnomes, except these have tips that are dyed in human blood. They will exsanguinate a human, large or small, old or young, smart or not, just to have its blood for color on its and its family's wardrobe. There is only one way to escape the clutches of the goblin, and that is to hand over to it what it most desires. However, since most people who are in the woods, regardless of the reason, are not usually wearing much jewelry and aren't carrying any gold, in most cases at least, they're as good as gone once these inherently evil fae folk have them in their sights. Many humans, especially children, end up goblins in the end.

It seems, though they are everywhere and anywhere you find thick woods and forest areas, there's one particular place on earth where goblins are becoming a serious problem. The goblin population is growing exponentially. Could there also be a missing child crisis? Would we ever really know? With the way the media and the powers that be, whoever "they" may be, tend to selectively report on all things paranormal and/or super-natural?

In 2012 in Zimbabwe, a pack of goblins, all in groups of two, ran into a classroom full of schoolgirls and sent them running, screaming out of the room when they not only started trying to snatch anything sparkly and shiny off the girls, but then started to transform and turn into baboons. Actual baboons! Think about this for a minute, because honestly, it's a bit genius. Who has more glittery and sparkly belongings than school-aged girls? Goblins, as previously mentioned, aren't usually so smart, except when emboldened by their numbers. Meaning, when they know if they should decide to work together, which they abhor doing, that their numbers will far surpass yours, they will attack and won't stop until they grab anything and every-thing that glitters and shines.

In some cultures and legends, including those in Zimbabwe and the surrounding areas of that region, goblins are known to be even more sinister than we initially would have ever thought if we are from the United States, Canada or even the UK. While our perception of them is as stated above, that they are greedy and will go after your children, which is horrible enough and probably one of the worst and most frightening things any of us could ever imagine, many of the legends from South Africa and surrounding areas have goblins invading marital beds and demanding sexual favors, both from the men and the women and sometimes from both as a couple. Usually they will use the couple's children as a kind of ransom, held over the heads of the husband and wife in order to get them to comply with their deviant sexual desires. Goblins are neither male nor female and also are both. While this may not make much sense to you, maybe it isn't supposed to. This is just one of the many things which we as humans and not a part of the fairy realm could ever really be able to understand. Many of us rely on science while many of them rely on magic. If this sort of bedroom encounter should ever happen to you, do everything you can to fight because they are nothing if not liars, and regardless of if you comply or not, most likely after they get what they want from you, they will still go after your child or children.

CHAPTER ELEVEN

THE GREEN CHILDREN OF WOOLPIT

Fairies live in another realm, and this is perhaps why they can't be so clearly defined all the time like we humans can be. For example, we all identify as human, but some may also identify as our nationality too. The fae don't work like this, and this is mainly the reason we have such a hard time distinguishing one from another as we do. During their monthly celebrations in the berry patches, along the streams and hills in the deepest darkest depths of the forests, while drinking magic wine and beer and doing their mating and celebrating, one species may in fact mate with another, creating a whole other type of being altogether. This is where some people think Sasquatch comes into play or who knows what else is lurking out there we might come to encounter someday, depending on how far the fae go on the nights when the moon is just right and all care goes out the window.

The element they are attached to or given dominion over is the one and only thing that never changes. Their magic is usually intertwined with that specific element and therefore will be much weaker or perhaps nonexistent if their particular element should be far away when they're trying to work their magic. For example, should you encounter a water sprite, think fast and run as far as you can away from the water as long as it's following you. Normally a fairy, regardless of species, will not want to travel farther than the magic of their element reaches. However, they don't want to risk a human going back to other humans and telling about the encounter. Then the rest of us will know, for absolute fact, that they do indeed exist.

I want to take a step back now and discuss another, much more popular type of fairy and perhaps the first type many of us came to know as children, again, while reading "fairy tales."

There are many different legends of the pixie. There is so much debate over what the name means, where it came from and, also, where the legends of these tiny creatures even began that to even try to get a straight answer is impossible. Let's focus instead on what their connection could be, if any, to the missing phenomenon. The earliest version of the story "The Three Little Pigs" was published in 1853 and actually had three little pixies in place of the pigs. The legend of these fae go back much further than that, however. Though pixies could be responsible for any number of the strange and mysterious vanishings in the woods, they, like many other fae we have learned about so far, are extremely fond of little children and will go out of their way very far to lure them into some form of play. In fact, it's said their favorite way to do this is to disguise themselves as a bundle of rags, presumably so a child who doesn't know any better will come along and pick the rags up, allowing the pixie to transform right before their very eyes.

Generally you will hear that the pixie is friendly and helpful towards humans, especially the children, for the most part. However, I tend to believe otherwise. It seems foolish, after all we've learned, to even consider trusting ANY species of fairy should we happen to cross paths with one. The way pixies look will also vary greatly depending on where you are getting your information, with one thing always remaining the same: they are teeny tiny.

Besides hiding in or even pretending to be rags, they are absolute pests. Remember all of the stories we've been coming across lately about climbers just randomly unattaching from their safety harnesses and falling hundreds of feet to their doom? Or perhaps the people who are confused and wandering, for whatever reason, through the woods and found days later at the bottom of a cliff? While some have survived these falls, it should make one wonder if perhaps a pesky little pixie had set their sights on something the human had that it wanted, and started buzzing about the person's head and face and made them stumble off the cliff. Once the human is down, whether passed out or deceased matters very little to them, they will then go through the human's pockets and possessions and take whatever it wants and leave the rest.

It's said they like to make their homes in shoes, which many find most interesting considering how many people who disappear in the woods who are gone forever, with all that's left behind being their sneakers. Think about it, if you're going to build a home for you and your family, you want it to be sturdy and able to stand up to the elements of nature. Does it make sense then perhaps that a large sneaker or boot, which a human would use for hunting or hiking or climbing, would do just these things for a tiny little fairy if they made their home out of it? Obviously a sandal would hold no interest to them if we are thinking along these lines.

Because there is no one single place or story of origin for any type of fae species, it stands to reason, at least to some, that this must be proof that throughout the world over, at one time or another, someone has come across a fairy. The nature of their encounter and the species with which their path has crossed are how each of these types of creatures got not only their name and reputation, but their entire legend.

Another very interesting fact about fairies, which is true regardless of the race, is that they have visible auras just like humans. The difference, though, is that mostly all humans are able to see it. This could well be why there is all of the confusion about what the creature was wearing. Perhaps if they're a breed that is known to wear green, but they have a red aura, this is what is causing the confusion. It stands though that most of them, regardless of breed, have a gray aura. The aura of mischief and misbehavior. The darker the gray, the meaner and nastier the breed. Remember we are speaking of the mostly unknown, the aura of the fae. Therefore the colors of the human aura and those of the fae vary greatly and mean completely different things.

There is one very well-known story of a brother and sister fae, of still unknown species, that has resurfaced since the creation of YouTube videos and interest has risen in fairies and everything about them. Most people who are familiar with the story, however, haven't yet put two and two together to realize that this is in fact a story or legend, depending on what you believe, of actual fairies. Remembering that they are not all tiny in size, I remind you of the story of the green children of Woolpit. For over nine centuries this story has been capturing the interest of many people who come across it, both those who believe in the fae and otherwise.

Just the general strangeness of it and the fact that it is mostly known to be a real encounter or true story makes people absolutely enamored with and fascinated by the tale of the brother and sister who randomly showed up in this village in England, speaking a language nobody had ever heard and which still allegedly cannot be interpreted to this day, wearing clothing made out of material no one had ever seen before or since, and having skin the color of bright green leaves. Skin the color of the leaves on trees when they first rebloom in the springtime. These children were confused by the most basic of things. Even the food they were offered seemed to have them absolutely bewildered, and all they would consume were raw beans. They ate nothing but these beans for months on end, but in almost all other ways began to adapt to the way of life in the village. They remained silent except to speak their unknown language amongst themselves but were otherwise seeming to be adapting well to what had to be a very dramatic change considering where it's said they came from. (We will get to that in a minute.)

It strikes many as odd, however, that upon being baptized, the boy almost immediately died. Could this be because a Christian baptism goes against the very nature of the fae and their magic? After her brother passed away and was given a Christian burial, the little girl started thriving. She learned to speak English, began eating like a normal human being and even lost her green skin color eventually. There finally came a time when she was able and felt comfortable enough to tell the villagers her story. According to the girl, she and her brother were from a place called "St. Martin's Land." Everything in this place, including the people, was green. The two were out herding their green cattle and heard a strange sound, like a bell ringing. She said they immediately became confused and disoriented and were compelled to start following the sound. This, she says, is how they ended up in their village. One minute they were in their homeland and the next this strange English town. Like the blinking of an eye.

Could they have accidentally and unknowingly stepped through a portal? Let's take a minute here to ponder whether or not these two actually knew, yet, that they were fairies.

Perhaps they are of a strange race or breed that has no actual use for or interest in us humans and didn't feel it necessary to tell their children about us and our world or realm. Maybe these particular types are just as fearful of us and our "magic" as we are of them, and the children had only heard of us in their own mixed up and backwards version of "fairy tales". "Beware the humans and their realm at all costs." Are there fairies who, for whatever reason, have no magic left and live a simple and mundane life such as the ones we humans lived centuries ago? Are they unsure of or trying to prove OUR existence? Maybe, at least that's what many who know better believe about this particular story.

The girl, who was given the Christian name Agnes, became known as ill-mannered and rude eventually as she tired of life in not just this village but this realm as well. No matter how hard she tried, she never could even come close to finding her way back home, and some say even blamed the English villagers for the death of her beloved brother. She never heard that bell again and eventually married and settled down to have a family, though not in Woolpit, but in a surrounding village. She never returned to Woolpit and is said to have died an old widow, bitter and angry about the life she loved so much, which was forever changed and taken from her, for unknown reasons. I wonder if, in even just a few of the many missing persons cases that happen in the woods, someone hears and is compelled to follow the sound of a strange bell and perhaps ends up in a tiny little outdated village called "St. Martin's Land," where everyone is green and from which there is no return.

Perhaps, though weak, whatever species of fae who lost two children to our human realm, their magic is strong enough to exact their revenge today. Maybe this is one of the reasons we "lose" so many children to the unknown wilderness.

I also wonder if children go missing more because perhaps they are less able to capture what is happening to them. Though there has yet to be any evidence found that's possibly been captured on a person who has gone missing's phone or camera or whatever kind of tech they may have on them, it's even less likely to happen, in my opinion, to a small child. Most adults, as far as I know, bring cameras and phones and other types of recording equipment so they can capture the beauty of nature, this makes the hunt and final capture that much harder for whatever predator is hunting them at that moment. Makes sense to me that a small child, a toddler perhaps who doesn't have access to or know how to use these technological devices, would make the perfect prey. Especially when one is in a hurry.

CHAPTER TWELVE

EVIDNETIARY PROOF

We talk a lot about technology nowadays and the fact it's near impossible to know if photo or video of alleged "evidence" of the existence of not just fairies but anything and everything else people have claimed to have encountered in the woods in the past few decades are real because of things like editing software and filter apps. When speaking about true crime and forensics, as we do a lot on my channel and throughout YouTube in general, we learn that, as a society, there is no better proof found at a crime scene than DNA.

Some skeptics have speculated that if fairies were real, surely there would be something left over from them, as not all species are said to be immortal. If many of them were, then why would they be so concerned and overly protective of their species as a whole? While we know by now that elves need human DNA every few generations in order to survive as a race, and we are also well aware that there are some breeds who replace their own sickly children with our healthy ones in order to maintain their survival, we don't know much of any of this, or really much of anything at all when it comes to the fae as fact. This includes whether or not any species are immortal. It would stand to reason to some that if a fairy were to die, regardless of species or race, there would be a protocol to get rid of the evidence of the body somehow. Perhaps magically disintegrating it or even somehow transporting it back to their own realm so no humans can verify their existence and then choose to go hunting for them. Despite their magic, there are many types of fae who are just as afraid of encountering us as we are of them, after all.

There is a man in Wilmington, North Carolina, United States, who in 2017 came across something incredibly strange yet also extremely fascinating. James Cornan was hiking in the Rocky Mountains and stumbled across a falcon's nest. When he looked inside, surely he did a double take, as he couldn't believe what his eyes had seen the first time. Had he actually seen what he thought he had? James picked up the anomalous object and took some pictures. The rest, as they say, is history, and the photos have since been causing quite a stir and a very hot debate as to what it was he actually found. Those of us familiar with fairies will say with certainty he indeed found the tiny skeleton of a pixie. There seems to be no other explanation for it, though skeptics are still scratching their heads and grasping at straws to come up with one.

Could it be possible at least, that before other pixies

were able to get to their deceased friend, a falcon swooped down and grabbed what it thought was a small animal and brought it back to its nest for its young to play with or feast upon? Could the bird have swooped it right out of the air? Who could ever know? There are just too many unknowns to ever say anything for sure when discussing the fae and the missing, let alone the two subjects together and how they may or may not be connected. Some evidence, though not undeniable, is at the very least unexplainable, and James' "fairy skeleton' is just one of those pieces of evidence.

Many people, even those who aren't very skeptical and believe in the existence of many things lurking in the woods, will turn up their noses at the notion and turn a blind eye to the fact that fairies exist. Even those who research things such as Bigfoot and even UFOs and aliens will absolutely write fairies and fae culture and any and all evidence of, and encounters with them, off as a bunch of nonsense. This, many believe, is exactly what the fae depend upon. The absolute refusal of some humans to even acknowledge their existence. That is, until it's too late.

This denial could very well be the difference between who goes into the woods and comes back out and who goes in and vanishes seemingly into thin air. Could the fairies somehow know this about a particular human? How easy it would be to sneak up on someone who won't even acknowledge your existence let alone be on the lookout for you. How little effort it would take to catch these people unaware and make them pay the ultimate price. Whether it's a breed that wishes to simply play and perhaps ends up getting too rough, or the ones who come searching for us and have the absolute intention of turning us into slaves or worse, it may be smart to listen to your human intuition when in the woods and forests, wherever in the world you are exploring them. Better safe than sorry, our mothers always said, so be sure to go prepared for anything and everything.

The fact of the matter is myths are called myths because they're untrue. People in ancient times used myths to explain away certain things, but also to give answers to children who at a certain stage in their toddler years ask "why" eight thousand or so times a day and won't stop until they get an answer. Many adults created them as well to try to scare their children into behaving or listening to them about one dangerous thing or another they couldn't otherwise get the child to stop being curious about. However, in our modern culture we definitely know better than to think these tall tales are true. Many people are still acting under the belief that fairies are myths, and this could be a fatal mistake to make. While by now we know it depends on the fairy that's encountered, it's a rare event to meet one whose presence you will leave completely unscathed. It seems even the ones who do us no harm there in the moment are highly likely to put some kind of curse on us for a later date or time. All I'm saying is this: many myths are based on much more than just an ounce of fact. Many are based on real experiences, had by thousands upon thousands of people, spanning across cultures and generations, which were orally handed down long before the written word existed. Just as I believe with all my heart that werewolves did in fact prey upon medieval villagers and that vampires will rip the throats out of either a farmer or his livestock, I believe that fairies existed long ago and still do today.

CHAPTER THIRTEEN

GONE TO SEE THE FAIRIES

Just because I believe many legends and fables are real, most of them deemed nonsense by other people my age, that doesn't at all mean that I don't approach everything with a healthy amount of skepticism. Usually I can tell almost immediately which alleged fairy encounters, both of modern day and of days long gone, are true and which ones are nothing more than a farce. There is one reported fairy incident in particular that still baffles me to this day. After all the research I've done, after all the photos I've seen of both fake and real fairies, there is one alleged fairy encounter, complete with "photographic" evidence, that I just can't seem to figure out.

In 1917 cousins Elsie Wright and Francis Griffiths returned home after playing in the water at Cottingley Beck in West Yorkshire. They were scolded for coming home soaking wet. Though they were allowed to visit this water spot, they were told time and again they weren't to play IN it. They were untidy and unkempt, and their parents weren't happy at all. It's alleged though that the girls' explanation for why they had been there in the first place was that they "had gone to see the fairies." Of course, everyone they told this to laughed at them, and the explanation was quickly written off as fantastical and perhaps a lame excuse for why they had misbehaved by swimming when they weren't supposed to. The imaginations of two young girls running wild.

Perhaps tired of being considered silly for something they knew was very real, they took Elsie's father's camera and went back to the babbling brook to photograph the proof they thought they needed to convince everyone else they weren't making it up and that the fairies were real. Arthur Wright decided to pacify his daughter and play along and developed the photos himself in his own darkroom in his house. Much to his, and everyone else but Elsie and Frances' surprise, the photos did in fact seem to show fairies. Francis was lying on the grass and gazing very peacefully up at the camera while Elsie snapped the photo and four tiny little, beautiful fairies (who seem to me to be of the pixie or perhaps even the sprite breed) fluttered about in front of her face. Arthur was convinced the images were fake. He was, after all, a professional photographer and knew there was no way the girls had actually caught fairies in a photo. Fairies are myths, legends, parts of the "fairy tales" he read to his daughter each night before bed. Polly, Elsie's mother, however, saw the images much differently and was awestruck and amazed that her daughter and niece had been able to capture still images of themselves frolicking with real-life fairies!

When I first saw these photos, it seemed very obvious to me that they were fakes, and not very good ones at that. Here is the confusing part though; there was another photograph taken that day, and this one was of Elsie standing next to a gnome. Again Arthur scoffed at the ridiculousness of it all while Polly was thrilled. Finally in 1919, Elsie's parents were able to get the photos looked at by a place called the "Theosophical Society" who investigated "the unexplained." Allegedly this society, who were supposed to be the best experts in the field of the unexplained at the time, at least in that area, were convinced the photos were real. Even Sir Arthur Conan Doyle was impressed by the images and urged the little girls to go back and get more evidence of the existence of fairies, in the form of more photographs, and bring them to him.

Of course, these photos of allegedly real fairies caused quite a stir, and soon everyone was talking about them. This means, of course, that the skeptics were also interested and were quick to point out all of the ways in which and the reasons why these photos simply couldn't be real. Mainly though they said that fairies weren't real and therefore couldn't possibly be caught on film.

In 1978, according to the Museum of Hoaxes, a Mr. James Randi claimed to have found images of the exact same fairies in the cousins' pictures in a book that belonged to Princess Mary. This book was published in 1915, so just a couple of years before the girls had claimed to have caught the tiny water elementals with Arthur Wright's camera.

In 1981 Elsie Wright came forward and admitted the photographs were indeed fake; however, her cousin Francis did no such thing and stuck to the original story that they were real and had been playing with the girls that day. When I looked at these allegedly real photographs, I have to admit, I myself wasn't convinced of their authenticity either. The thing that makes me wonder though is the fact that it is 2021, and still, as far as my research can tell, no one has been able to say with absolute certainty if the photos are real or fake.

England's fairies date back to the thirteenth century when historian Gervase of Tilbury first described them. Belief in fairies was so widespread that most people refused to mention them by name. Instead, they referred to them as "Little People" or "Hidden People." This tradition still lingers to this day, with many people all across the globe using these alternate names for the fae in general. It's very nonspecific for how many types of fairies actually exist, but I suppose if you are terrified of something and want to avoid it at all costs, which seems to be the case here, it's best not to think about how rampant they are. Though first mentioned by an Englishman and historian, the majority of the old legends and tales of the fae come from Ireland, with one fairy race in particular that seems to capture the interest of the public much more than any other, and, in my opinion one that is also much more not only believed in but celebrated. That's right, there is one fae species whose legend withstands the tests of time and spans across generations and countries. Whose legend is known throughout almost any and all countries, throughout the entire world over. Its colonization is said to have predated even the Celts in the lovely and enchanting Emerald Isle.

CHAPTER FOURTEEN

THE ELUSIVE LEPRECHAUN

In Ireland the most well-known and possibly most sought after fairy is the elusive leprechaun, this tiny little, rotund troublemaker who, if you're lucky enough to catch him, is said to be compelled to offer you three wishes. There is a story though about an Irish couple who caught a leprechaun on their farm. They were out tending their animals when they saw him running through their fields in his little green outfit, complete with gold belt buckle and pointy hat. The couple claimed that they did indeed catch the little guy, but the details on how they accomplished this magnificent feat are a bit fuzzy. What we do know, however, is that the couple claim to have been granted only one wish. Allegedly they couldn't think of just one thing they wanted more than anything, and their list of wishes was so long the leprechaun got impatient and fled without granting the wish. Alternatively, he is said to have told the couple to go and find the end of the rainbow where he kept his pot of gold hidden. That way, they would have enough money to buy whatever their hearts desired, and it would save him the trouble of having to wait around any longer. This is where the legend of the pot of gold at the end of the rainbow is said to have come from. As far as I could tell, this is one of the first stories ever told of a leprechaun with treasure at the end of a rainbow.

Leprechauns are just one of many types of fae that are said to have been banished to live their lives underground. The fact that there are no female leprechauns is the reason, some say, that they are so grumpy, greedy, selfish and solitary all of the time. Like the goblin, you will almost never see more than one leprechaun at a time. I try not to think of the logistics of how faeries such as the leprechauns procreate when there are only male members in their species.

Perhaps they unite with one or all of the all-female clans of fae, who are similarly known to be ornery, miserly and equally self-absorbed. The banshees, nixies and leanan sidhe are just a few of these all-female sorts. Leprechauns are supposedly the true natives of Ireland, the first to inhabit the beautiful land, allegedly descended from real Irish royalty, before being pushed out by the Celts.

Unfortunately for those of us who are looking for a pot of gold or to capture one of these mischievous old grumps, if you do not live in the Emerald Isle, you will be sorely disappointed because they can only be found there. In the rural areas, far away from even the most sparsely populated villages. Leprechauns not only despise people and other fae folk, but other leprechauns as well. This is most likely because of how untrusting they are said to be. They live very deep in underground caves, the entrances hidden as fox or rabbit holes. They will also make their homes in the hollows of a specific type of "fairy tree," perhaps this means it is hidden by magic, which makes it invisible to the human eye. The leprechaun has many talents that are virtually overlooked due to most people knowing that if you should capture one, he will be compelled to grant you three wishes. Be careful though, as they are great tricksters and supersmart wordsmiths and could have you regretting what you've wished for, each one more than the last.

They have a great love of music and are experts at playing instruments such as the fiddle, the Irish harp and the tin whistle, just to name a few. They love to dance as well, and they will hold parties and celebrations that will last for days on end. These parties, or "Celi's," are one of the few and extremely rare times you will see a leprechaun interacting with not only other leprechauns but also with fairies of every kind. All fae are welcome when these little men decide to throw a shindig. They are shoemakers by trade, and this just shows exactly how smart and resourceful they are when it comes to money, gold and business. We have talked so much about how fairies love to celebrate and dance, no matter what the occasion is or even if there is any occasion at all. They don't need an excuse. As famous Irish poet W. B. Yeats once said, "Because of their love of dancing, they will always need shoes." With the "they" in that statement meaning the fae. All of them, every single species and breed with the exception of so few, love to dance, sing, play music and celebrate. Yeats goes on to tell a story about a woman who was taken away by the fairies and who returned seven years later, missing all of her toes. She had allegedly danced them off! Yes, it's that serious! Perhaps this is why they venture above ground for these sometimes ritualistic parties and mating games. Perhaps as well, this is why it is so dangerous should you come across or accidentally lay your eyes on any of this!

CHAPTER FIFTEEN

THE FAE IN OUR MODERN WORLD

There is another theory I found very interesting that I came across first while researching for this book. It is similar to the children of Eve legend I told earlier, but different enough to make one scratch their head. With the Christian church being a supporter of the existence of fairies, at least for a time, I do wonder if the previous legend or this one is the one most accepted in Christian religious circles. The legend states that Jesus Himself turned some small children into fairies after their mother, Eve, attempted to hide them due to her shame over how many she had given birth to. At this time there were twenty children in all. Once Jesus transformed the children, they flew away and were never seen or heard from again. Nobody seems to know where they went. Perhaps this is how the legends of the fae became so widespread all over the world.

A Montgomeryshire minister whose name I couldn't find once postulated that God allowed the fae to appear only in times of great ignorance simply to convince doubters of the existence of an invisible world. A world beyond theirs, which they could neither see nor touch. In the beginning of this book I wondered why we are just now starting to see so much more of not just the fae but many other previously hidden supernatural beings and creatures, mainly in the woods. Is there something going on in the invisible worlds that surround us that is making the veil that much thinner that we can almost see right through it? Maybe that's it, or maybe the veil is actually lifting altogether. It could be that God Himself has ordered the fae specifically to show themselves. Why? Well, possibly because of all of the debate over whether or not they exist and all of the attention they're getting because of the ever growing number of sightings being reported in recent years. Their connection to the missing is also becoming more prevalent, and therefore people are beginning to take them and other supernatural supposed myths and legends more seriously. He wants to convince and remind people that there are invisible worlds all around us. To make the Earth a place of believing in things we can't see or reach out and touch. A world, maybe, of faith?

There is another theory that states that the fae are former angels who refused to choose a side during Lucifer's revolt. Because of their insolence, God damned them, and they were banished to the Otherworld, doomed to roam between heaven and hell for all of eternity. In the sixteenth century, during the Protestant Reformation of the Christian church, the belief that all fae folk were demons was made part of the church's belief system as a whole. Therefore anyone choosing to believe something different or, in some cases, to believe in the existence of them at all or to interact with them in any way was grounds for execution at the stake, burned as a witch. In the demonology texts written in the days of the witch trials, fairies were said to be one of the most prominently featured beings with whom the condemned had been performing black magic or practicing the dark arts.

This "Otherworld" that is said to be inhabited by fairies in many cultures was also associated with or even said to be "the land of the dead." Therefore it's often said that the spirits of our ancestors and even our deceased family members have moved on to this place and live in tandem with the fairies there to this very day. It's even said that the unbaptized souls of deceased children and infants are able to take the form of any fae and participate in any of their rituals and traditions. Does this mean they actually become a fairy? It is just my opinion that these souls are in fact able to somehow become certain types of fae species, though which ones I have no idea. I've yet to find much if any credible research on the subject. We have to always remember that the fae are an ancient race of beings, they are featured not just in modern-day society and our folklore, but they also play a prominent role in ancient legends as well.

They live a sort of metaphysical existence, yet are somehow still able to cross over into our world, the physical world. In ancient Greece there were gods and goddesses who ruled over everything, but it was nymphs who actually played the most important roles under these deities. These nymphs were mainly female, and caring for the earth was their main job. They took on many tasks, mainly in the garden tending flowers, helping the roots of the trees grow, thrive and come alive. The nymphs were even able to help out on a hot and muggy day with a cool breeze and some light rain when the immortals requested or when they saw a friendly and familiar human who needed to cool down. The nymphs didn't just do their work in the residential homes of familiar humans or on Mount Olympus where the immortals resided, but ruled over and cared for the forests and all of the animals in them as well.

Besides the female nymphs, there were the male satyrs, or silenos. This was a very small spirit of nature who was sometimes given the status of demigod. This was a very prominent title for an elemental or nature spirit, and it was hard for them to obtain, as they were known troublemakers. These little men had a body like a modern-day elf only with the tail of a horse, pointed elf ears, and a very prominent erection that is almost always exaggerated in drawings and the retelling of tales about them. They would do whatever task that was given to them; almost always it was overseeing a lesser entity or person's work. These supervisory positions ranged from overseeing the wine making to watching the kitchen and ensuring nobody double dipped a spoon in the ambrosia.

Another fae creature heavily discussed in Greek mythology is the siren. They were described in their literature as "half beautiful maiden and half bird," which as we know is quite different from what we think of today when we hear of a siren. Many people wrongly believe they are almost the same as a mermaid, but that isn't the case. This is a good example of how modern-day culture has seemingly gone out of its way to bastardize the ancient legends and myths. The sirens' singing attracted the sailors in their vicinity and led them straight to their doom. It's said that even if the sailors somehow survived the sirens' song, their fate would be death anyway. Legend has it that all of the sirens drowned when they stormed into the ocean all at once in a fit of rage when Odysseus somehow got by them without being tempted or lured by their beautiful songs. Many who study these things today, myself included, aren't so sure though, as there have been many reports in the years since the ancient Greeks and even in recent years, where the sirens have been heard throughout the ocean, all across the world. I wonder sometimes if this is the cause of seemingly random and unexplained drownings.

We incorporate these legends into our modern lives much more than we even realize. We have Brownies in our Girl Scout troops. We keep gnome statues in our yards and gardens, and some of us even go so far as to cultivate what we like to call "fairy gardens," which are made specifically to look like the landscapes we see in the contemporary literature that we call "fairy tales." These gardens are often quite small, and much of the time they are made with the intent of luring real fairies in and giving them a beautiful place to live, grow and play. I'm not sure if this is brilliant, silly or downright dangerous. I guess it could be considered any of these three ways. If it's to be considered brilliant, perhaps that's because what better way to get the fairies out of our woodlands and forests and get them to stop abducting and possibly killing off humankind?

It's also sort of silly because the fairies are the rulers of nature. Elemental spirits of nature, so what use would they have for such man-made dwelling places? I do believe, however, these "fairy gardens" are more dangerous than anything else as they trivialize the fae and even make a mockery of them. Trying to lure in something you know absolutely nothing about is never a good idea, and if people would do their research and be diligent, they would see that this is an accident or a purposeful incident waiting to happen. If they attract the wrong kind of fairy, all hell will break loose, and either they or someone they love could lose their life.

CHAPTER SIXTEEN

THE SHAPESHIFTING OGRE

Bringing us back to modern-day fairies and the missing, if you are still not convinced fairies are real, you don't even have to take my word for it. In fact, just look at a census taken in 2014, just seven years prior to this book being written. This census was on fairy sightings, and the results were shocking! Allegedly, according to the poll, which was carried out by the Faery Investigation Society, 450 fairy sightings were recorded in that year alone. On the word of these reports, not only are sightings and even personal encounters becoming more and more commonplace, the fairies we humans are coming up against are getting not only more malicious, but downright deadly. In my opinion, this only lends more credence in the way of evidence that one, fairies do exist, and two, they are responsible for a large number of disappearances and even deaths that are recorded as strange, suspicious or even unknown.

Throughout this book we have learned much about many different types of fae species.

Not only the ways in which they interact with and affect us humans on a daily basis but, also, what happens when we even accidentally come across them, or when they come hunting for us. I'd be remiss in my duties, however, if I were to neglect to mention another type of fae that has become quite popular in modern children's stories and fairy tales throughout the world. Once again though, they are being misrepresented, and this misrepresentation could end up posing a deadly threat were we or one of our children to just happen to come across one on an innocent hike or stroll through the woods.

Many of us have seen the movies where the cartoon ogre is nothing more than a big, green, sometimes dim-witted, friendly type of creature with whom you can have a good laugh or even a pleasant evening of dining and dancing. That is, if you could just handle the horrific stench they seem to constantly emanate and live within. While the foul odor and even the green skin are quite accurate, to think one could be anything more than a meal to any ogre would be a terrible mistake. They are not just bullies of humans though but of other, smaller fae species as well. They are adept at muscling other fairies out of not only their food and wealth but out of their homes too. Though usually having below average intelligence, they make up for it in muscle and nastiness. I mean the latter in more ways than one, but we will get to that.

Ogres are said to be descended from the now extinct giants and are incredibly large, both in height and girth. They are not, however, actual giants, as many tend to believe. A height of twelve to fourteen feet tall is the average, give or take a few inches. They walk on their hind legs, regardless of their size or stature. Some species even have one eye or an extra appendage or two, though very rare. The ogre stands out as the only race of fae creatures that have these extra or even noticeably missing body parts.

While pretty much anything they own has most likely been stolen from other fae creatures or humans, they almost always end up having their belongings stolen from them, by either of the aforementioned races, due to their vanity and extreme laziness. They are known to only be awake a couple of hours a day and therefore don't usually have much time left after hunting for their food. This makes them very easy to avoid but deadly should you cross their paths, I reiterate, even by accident. The main thing that makes them so incredibly dangerous to us humans is their taste for human flesh and blood. It's said human blood is akin to our finest champagne and our flesh like succulent meat, pulled right from the bone if necessary. Not only do they use us as snacks and meals for sustenance, but they have no remorse, and all of the begging and pleading in the world would get you no sympathy or reprieve. Once you have crossed the path of an ogre, you are doomed to become their meal. Though usually wasteful, there is one exception in that they put us humans to good use. They even make their houses from our bones and anything left over they cannot eat or drink. Sometimes, the bodies of smaller humans, like children and even infants, end up as playthings or "dolls" for the ogre's children.

They have no issue with the stench of rotting flesh or

decay, so this is actually a wonderful and precious gift to the child ogre.

Just like their goblin cousins, ogres are known to be shape-shifters. The difference though is this: although they can shift into any person or animal they want, they are then beholden to the limitations of each. Also, they must have already laid eyes on the person or animal whose form they are choosing to steal and can only remain in the body for a very limited amount of time. If it is choosing to become a human in order to fool, say, the person's family into coming with it into the woods, it would have to do it quickly, as it would be hard-pressed for time. Humans can almost always outrun the giant ogres in their regular form, as they are morbidly obese, extremely tall and unbelievably stupid. Their magic is said to be so weak it's almost nonexistent. Shape-shifting is basically the only devilry it has left. So slovenly and foolish are the ogres that they have lost all knowledge of the ancient magics given to them so long ago. While almost all of the other fae species literally ARE magic, this is not true for goblins or ogres. In my opinion it's because they are an abomination; put plainly they are just too evil to be allowed to hold something so sacred.

They are also solitary creatures, and except to mate, it would be almost unheard of to see more than one in the same place, especially dwellings. Even the male and female go their separate ways after breeding, for such a fiend is the male he would eat his own young in order to try to entice the female to mate again, as her main goal is to procreate. They can be found living in any form of abandoned building or cave in any forested area or even local woods. As wonderful as it would be to think of them only in lands far away and in tiny little straw huts, their massive size and even more gigantic ego disables them from making their home anywhere they feel isn't fit for a king, or queen for that matter. Large bear caves or other possible abandoned structures found in the woods will do for a dwelling place. Anything massive and deserted in general. Despite popular belief, ogres can and will choose abandoned hospitals and institutions, mansions or plantation homes for themselves, provided civilization is far enough away. They need humans for food, remember, so it shouldn't come as a surprise at all that they don't shy away from sparsely populated areas where there are at least some humans around. Sightings of them have been reported the world over, even in recent years. The problem is the reports are very uncommon, since almost any human who should be so unlucky as to encounter one will surely end up filling its belly and decorating its home.

If you should be out in the woods, for whatever reason, watch yourself and anyone in your party very closely. Remember they can shape-shift into human form, any that they have previously laid their eyes on, even for just a second. If you think someone has been possessed or overtaken by an ogre, all you have to do is look at their eyes. If the eyes are suddenly yellow or have a yellowish glow to them, you are dealing with an ogre who has taken the form of a human. It should be easy to tell, as they only come out in what is the middle of the night in human time. Sometimes the person whose form an ogre has chosen to take will suddenly become sick and confused, this leads us right back to the missing in the woods.

How many times now have we discussed the sudden confusion and nausea that usually comes immediately before a person either goes missing for a time or disappears forever? If we think along the lines of these horrific ogres when thinking of fairies, maybe we shouldn't go exploring any place that is abandoned or unoccupied. Between these savage breeds of fairies and any and everything else lurking about, it shouldn't even be a surprise anymore how many people go missing not only in the woods but in urban and suburban areas as well. Most people, even those who absolutely believe in fairies, don't even know that there are some who do in fact leave the woods and forests. The ogres and goblins... The non-elementals. They are not attached to any one element, the only ones of their kind. Goblins, ogres and trolls, oh my! Be careful where you roam, as you never know what's lurking.

CHAPTER SEVENTEEN

ONE-S DED ARRANGEMENTS

While we have only scratched the surface so far in the very vast sea of information available on the fae, and all of the connections I've been able to make between them and the missing people all over the world's woods and forests, there is still so much more to learn. While there are many "experts" out there who have their own theories and thoughts on how you should and shouldn't behave should you ever encounter a fairy or other sort of fae folk, I will give you here some lesser known information that may be helpful should you ever come across one or a few of these "little people." (Or big people, depending upon the species and breed, which we will get to a bit later on.) Know that, while the alleged encounters previously mentioned seem to show a more benevolent side to fairies and their legends, they are often known to be much more evil and complicated to pin down from one country to the next. Most, however, state that these creatures are master manipulators, and should you come across them, never, under any circumstances, enter into any kind of deal or arrangement with them. They are not only wonderful and skilled connivers, but also masters of language and are known to find loopholes and use linguistic trickery to fool you into dealing with them, only for you to later realize you never stood a chance at getting what you wanted or what you were supposed to receive while the creature gets anything and everything out of the deal that they originally set out to. They will always be the ones to benefit, mostly at the detriment of the person they are dealing with, especially if the other party is a human.

Here are just a few of the rules of engagement when it comes to these legendary and magical beings. Never insult them, and no matter what, be polite. Try your best not to anger them, as this is how most people are said to end up disappearing. If you ever get the feeling you are being watched by something you can't see or get a sudden feeling like you aren't supposed to be where you are, turn around and leave immediately. Though they love presents and gifts, choose carefully what you leave for them because if whatever you've chosen isn't sweet, your positive gesture of kindness and respect can very quickly turn into something very negative and very dangerous.

Never use the words "thank you" or "I'm sorry." It is much more acceptable and safer for you to use the words "I appreciate that" or "pardon me," for one admits fault while the other acknowledges a wrong may have been done and simply asks for forgiveness. "Thank you" will put you in their debt, while "I appreciate that" will simply express gratitude. The fae are known to speak in riddles, and there's almost always some kind of hidden meaning underneath what they're saying, so always pay close attention and listen carefully, lest you become one of the missing or another statistic in a book just like this one. The list is endless on how these creatures can fool and trick you, leading you into your own abduction and possible disappearance. My hope is that when you are through with this book, you will be much better and more safely able to navigate the woods and forests you choose to hike, hunt and/or camp in. My hope is to help others avoid the same tragic fate as many of the missing, both those who have returned and those who never stood a chance.

To really get to the bottom of what the differences are with each species and breed of the fae and figure out a way to just avoid all of them altogether but also be protected with knowledge and truth about all of this is, as well, the main goal and intention of this book. I believe there is something much more sinister afoot than a little sprinkle of sparkly dust putting us humans to sleep for a little bit, and the goal of the sleep is never just some rest. No, there's much more going on here with these mostly ornery, not so helpful little beasts and the things they do to confuse and put humans down for a little catnap so they can steal them away, taking them from here, which is known, to somewhere unknown. If only it were as simple and cutesy and fun as a little shimmer of glitter dust and all of our troubles immediately disappear. In reality though, it's more like sudden and total confusion, which causes unrelenting panic as the hapless victims of these clever little tricksters who, in the blink of an eye, find themselves completely lost. Turned around, dazed and confused as to what just happened and where they were. Sometimes days are lost, sometimes longer, and sometimes, the victim is gone forever, fallen prey to whatever game the fairy decided to make them a part of. Completely helpless, alone and afraid. Screaming at the top of their lungs but then realizing, with horror I'm sure, that they have no voice.

As I mentioned briefly earlier in the book, these "little people" aren't always so little.

While the majority of them are said to be four feet tall or shorter, some are said to be as tall as ten feet. What about all of the clusters of missing people turning up all over the world that have recently come to light and the connections made to what we know about the fae? Boulder fields and circles of stone should never be disrupted. This is said to be where they live and play, and you do not want to disturb a fairy creature's resting place. As we know by now, they do not take kindly to anything they see as disrespectful, and as such sensitive little beings, that's most anything they haven't granted you permission to do. Do not even approach such places unless you are prepared for the possible fate that lies ahead of you if you do. After all, how could you be granted permission to do anything by entities that you cannot see with your human eyes unless they should allow you to look upon them, which they most often do not do. If they should ever grant you this permission, to gaze upon them, that is, be wary, for they almost always have some trick up their sleeves. If you do not come prepared with the aforementioned gifts of sweets, alcohol and/or tobacco, do not expect a very generous or hospitable welcome. In fact, if you do not bring such gifts, I suggest you stay away altogether, as this will certainly anger them, and they carry such great wrath for being so very tiny in size for the most part. It's said, "The smaller the fae, the greater the fury!"

There seems to be an inordinate amount of people who go missing while picking berries or near berry bushes. You may be struck with an unexplained and suddenly desperate need to go and fill several baskets with the plump and juicy fruit of which there are too many varieties to name. We see all the time in movies about survival in the deep woods and forests that you should always beware of eating berries to stay alive, for they might just be poisonous and ironically the very thing that ends up killing you off. However, has anyone ever stopped to think about why these berries are poisonous? If, perhaps, they were made so by something we can't understand?

Struck by a sudden and irresistible impulse to go and gather the fresh fruit you are most likely being lured by the fae to your doom. They like to play, after all, and among the bushes and brambles of the berry patches is where they are known to do their dancing and mating. This is also where they embrace the earth and sing with all of their heart, sometimes fully visible and most of the time at least audible to humans who are unfortunate enough to be in their general vicinity at these times. If you should catch a glimpse of a dance or hear even the slightest whisper of a tune—turn back, for they do not like to be disturbed. Again, they only like to be seen or heard if it is their choice. If they should feel that choice was taken away from them, then there will be consequences. Could this be the fate of so many who have disappeared among a berry patch in recent years? My advice would be to just go to the produce section of your local grocery store or farmers' market for your berry needs. They may not be as fresh as if you picked them yourself, but at least you won't be lost forever.

Fairies are known more for when it comes to disappearing objects or "things" than taking humans and putting them "somewhere else," either for a little while or for the rest of forever. If you aren't extremely careful in choosing which paths you take and follow while out in the woods, you could just happen upon a fairy procession. They mostly take part in this particular activity by the light of the full moon, and should you stumble upon it, whether accidentally or on purpose, you may just be able to escape back to your family and all that you love, feeling a sense of safety and that all is well. Perhaps you think maybe you dodged a bullet, so to speak, only to find that within days of the encounter you have completely lost your mind. Fairies have powerful magic, regardless of species, race or breed. Their abilities are quite substantial, and they are well skilled in all they practice and do. You will never escape so easily unless it is a part of the game, whichever they are playing. Though that depends on which type you have come across, of course. Just one look into their eyes for a split second and your senses could be completely lost forever, with your physical body being wherever you are, while your mind is viewing their world and lives through their eyes, only you cannot decipher the difference.

CHAPTER EIGHTEEN

PROTECTING OURSELVES

My main hope for and goal of this book is to enlighten you, the reader. It's a fact that most people go into the woods thinking they are prepared "for anything and everything." When in fact that couldn't be further from the actual truth. What do we always hear? Be sure to bring a compass, a map, a personal locator beacon and perhaps even a firearm. (Provided you are trained to use one.) The fact of the matter though is that not a single one of these things could help you should you encounter a fairy or other magical being. I'm not saying being prepared with the above mentioned things isn't a smart idea, because it absolutely is. However, statistically speaking, you're much more likely to die in the crashing of a small plane over a national park than from a bear attack or snake bite while inside. The supernatural and even paranormal beings that seem to have overtaken our natural woods and forest areas in the recent past, and in centuries before the modern invention of most of the aforementioned safety objects, are absolutely and totally impervious to bullets.

If I were to go into the woods for any reason at all, even for a day hike, while I might consider bringing some or all of the "usual" items to help and defend and guard against becoming a statistic, I would certainly make sure my backpack contained a few other things as well. The aforementioned candy or sweets, tobacco and liquor gifts would be the first things I bring along with me during any trips into the woods or vacations to national parks.

St. John's Wort is also great to have on hand, as it is said to be the best possible plant to use for protection against not only fairy attacks but from their magic as well, and just having it on your person, even if not visible, will keep you safe.

If you are lucky enough to have access to four-leaf clovers, it would be a good idea, too, to bring these with you, as having them in your possession will enable you to see any species of fae that may be near you, even if they have rendered themselves invisible. The trick here though, for our part, is to carry many. Each four-leaf clover allows us to see the invisible fairy, but only once. So carrying a bunch of them will keep the fairies visible for as many as you have brought with you. Again, these don't need to be seen by the fairy, they just have to be in your possession while traveling near them. There are some legends that even allege that having the clovers will not only allow you to view the invisible lurkers, but will give you a sort of second sight. One with which you could even see through fairy "glamors" and tricks. This is especially useful if traveling alone to protect you from being taken in by the fae when they want to abduct you and use their magical trickery and mirages to do so.

If your children happen to be playing in the woods either by themselves or with you by their sides, it would be wise to tuck some daisies into their pockets, as this is said to prohibit the fairies from abducting them altogether, though why or how any of these things work is beyond me.

Yeast-risen bread is said to repel some fairies and provide a gift to others whom you may be able to fend off by giving it as a food offering, perhaps even a peace offering to those you may have accidentally offended. Keeping this with you at all times as well serves a double purpose.

If you want any fairies who may be hanging around or possibly living in your backyards or gardens to refrain from playing mischievous or even downright evil tricks on your family or even your animals, an old Welsh tradition could be just the thing. In this tradition you are to leave a slice of bread and a saucerful of milk outside either on your front or back porch or deck. If you are looking to get the fairies to help you in some way, add some honey, cheese or fresh berries, and this will tell them you are a friend who needs their assistance.

Salt in general, because of its association with purity, makes an excellent tool against any and almost all other-worldly beings. It will keep all fairies away and repel them, but it is especially useful against the more evil races. Spreading salt against any threshold or along all of your windowsills is said to keep away not only the fae but also ghosts, spirits and/or demons of all kinds. Sprinkling your livestock or farmhands' food with salt is also a very good idea, as it will repel the fae and therefore disable them from being able to either steal the food or just the nourishment it contains, which they love to do because no one would ever be the wiser.

There is also a flower called the marsh marigold, which was fastened into a wreath and hung above barn doors at night to prevent the horses from being ridden to exhaustion by fairies in the night while the humans slept peacefully and unknowingly in their beds.

Sprinkling oatmeal over your clothing before heading out to explore the woods and forests works very well too, as does just keeping a handful of it in your pocket.

The very best and most commonly known and used item that is useful in preventing anything horrible coming your way from any type of fae species, race or breed is good old, trusty iron. Something as simple as keeping an iron nail in your pocket would prevent them from carrying you away. This is exactly the kind of thing I believe personally the "experts" should be telling people to be packing for a camping or hiking trip, right along with all of the above mentioned and more commonly known "survival gear."

Hanging iron shears on the wall near your infant's crib or small child's bed is said to keep away the fairies who are looking to swap their changelings. If you abide by the old legends that claim a horseshoe over the door or any entrance point into your home will keep evil away, that's smart. Remember, however, that to specifically keep the fae from coming anywhere near your home, the horseshoe must be placed in the shape of a C, to symbolize the crescent moon.

Steel, being created by processed iron, would also be a very effective weapon or tool to use against the fae and their magic. Many legends say that a fairy injured or cut by a steel blade will either be unable to heal or will heal very slowly. Some of these tales go so far as to say the wound will slowly poison the fairy and they will actually die. They will cease to exist not just in this realm, but in theirs as well. In fact, steel and/or iron weapons are the only things on earth that can actually kill a fairy. Again, I apologize I cannot offer you much by way of explanation into how or why these things work so well, but can only assure you that they do. Even if you don't believe it, wouldn't you rather be safe than sorry?

CONCLUSION

When it comes to all of the missing people in the woods these days, vanishing without a trace and perhaps being lost somehow to history and legends, it isn't easy for me to tell you that fairies aren't the only answer. Simply put, they are just one of many. What brought my attention to the fae was how much their lives and even just tales about them seem to coincide with what we know about the people who go missing in this way. After all, the fae don't only abduct people and keep them forever or kill them. As we have seen, they will take a specific human, for a specific reason, for a very specific amount of time. These are all things that play a role in whether or not you come back, and the condition you are in if and when you do. How many of the supposedly missing are actually just gone from here? Taken from our realm and brought into the realm of the fae. A realm of magic and things beyond those that we as mere humans could possibly even begin to comprehend.

I even find myself referring to the "problem" of so

many people going missing every day from places that are supposed to be there for our amusement, fun and recreation as a problem that has only started coming to light in more recent years. In all actuality though, this couldn't possibly be further from the truth. I find myself constantly wondering if these things have always been going on, since the beginning of our time here on this planet, but only recently has it all been brought to light? If not full belief, then at least more interest in things like the fae and their world, a realm that either surrounds ours or is parallel to it, becomes more and more common with each and every disappearance. When small children turn back up hundreds of miles away from where they were last seen, a few weeks or even a month later, after vanishing from right under their parents' noses and seemingly in the blink of an eye, it's becoming less far-fetched when the child tells of some magical being who took them somewhere else for a little while. Somewhere "other."

It's true there are too many supernatural entities lurking about in the woods for me to even name here, had I written a name for every word in this entire book. Why has my focus been solely on the fae then, if there are so many threats to humanity itself and to us humans who explore the beautiful and unknown nature of our planet? Well, because I believe, personally, that the fae are the most prominent and the most dangerous things to be reckoned with out there. There isn't a single weather event, state of confusion, bizarre encounter, or even way of being found deceased that can't be traced back to at least one and possibly many more species of fairy. The information is out there and becoming more and more readily available as the disappearances and strange things go on happening, over and over again. Day after day and year after year, and every single time it does, there are even more people who refuse to stand idly by and listen to what they're being told because it just isn't making much sense anymore. Please, prepare for the fae when traversing nature. Even if only in your backyard.

Educate your children and loved ones. Even if they scoff and/or mock you, the time may come when they have an encounter or experience just as you had warned them they would, and at least they will know what to do. Guard and protect yourself and anyone who happens to be with you from these mystical and evil creatures, always remembering that not just their magic but they, too, are ancient. Possibly predating humanity itself.

Please do not even go near berry patches. Keep some form of iron on you at all times and go out of your way to find some four-leaf clovers. Never simply dismiss what you don't understand or seek what you can't possibly comprehend. Even after all of this writing and researching I have done, I have still only been able to scratch the surface with what I have reported to you here. I will continue on my quest for truth and answers and never stop reporting to the masses what it is I find out there. When out in groups, please try not to be the first or the last in line, and never, under any circumstances, let small children or the elderly out of your sight. If you are especially smart, then please never hike or camp alone. Remember too the fae are extremely skilled at making things appear to be what we deem a simple accident. Tragic, but accidental still. Don't let your guard down for a moment, not even in your own backyards and gardens, and never, ever play around or near circles of stones or rings of mushrooms. Do not mock the fae or any other supernatural creature you think could be lurking in the shadows around you out there in the wide-open spaces of our world.

Fairies have been found in every single culture, on every single continent and in every single country's myths and legends for generations. Before even the written word was invented. For centuries we have searched for answers and the truth, and when we haven't been able to come up with anything that makes sense, we have seemingly and suddenly turned to what we used to think of as nonsensical. Centuries ago the fae were a regular part of our everyday lives, and as humans we sometimes even worked hand in hand with them, coming to rely upon each other. Forming if not some sort of bond, then at least a mutual understanding of each other, if only for a short time. It's true we live in a much different world now, and some loyalties have since shifted, but I think as long as we stay prepared and vigilant, and as long as we keep searching for answers, we will maybe one day be able to prevent at least some of these disappearances and deaths that are happening so frequently all across the globe. There is only so much we are able to convince ourselves is coincidence before we no longer accept what is being told to us and start looking in more unconventional places.

So the next time you are out and about in your country's woods and forests, be sure to keep all of this in mind.

Be sure to bring more with you than the few items the average modern-day survivalist and nature expert recommends. Perhaps you should even keep this book with you in case you should find yourself in a bind or, worse, in the bad graces of one of the fae folk. They can be quite unforgiving, remember. My hope is that now your eyes will be more open and you will feel more enlightened when heading outdoors, for whatever reason. Gone for us are the days of the Disneyfied fairy, as we all should know by now that it's more like a Brothers Grimm Tale out there. This is just one part of the overwhelming and extensive research I have been able to gather about the missing and the fae. This is just a tiny portion of my theory about the fae and the missing. Be kind to each other. Go in grace, and always be sure to respect the unknown, for you never know what is near you and wishing to cause harm, just waiting for a reason to strike.

ABOUT THE AUTHOR

Gemma Jade was born and raised in Passaic County, New Jersey and has always felt drawn to the paranormal and supernatural world. She saw her first full bodied apparition at the age of four and was more interested in than terrified of it. Once she was old enough she started to seek answers. Gemma is of Native American and Irish descent and was fascinated by the old legends from both countries. She first encountered the fairies and their magic when she was 7 and her paternal grandmother from the Irish old country would tell her of the myths and legends of "the Little Ones." Gemma was and continues to be lured by the unknown. She is also a clairvoyant and clairsentient psychic and credits this to her native American blood. She currently resides in Morris County, New Jersey.

Gemma has taken her research and search for all things paranormal, supernatural and unexplained to her youtube channel titled simply Gemma Jade. She has joined with Steve Stockton to livestream and communicate with other like minded individuals who are searching for the truth. They talk a lot about the missing in the woods, and of course the fae. Gemma's focus on her channel is also to bring light to missing person's cases happening all over the world both inside and out of the woods. She has even given a platform to her viewers where they cannot only feel safe in telling their own encounters, but also where they can communicate with like minded individuals in her community.

Join Gemma on her channel here: https://www.youtube.com/c/GemmaJadeYT